What If Jesus…

…meets us in the good, the bad, and the messy?

"What if Jesus…" questions for authentic participation.

Dr. Greg Williams and Mark Mounts MA, LPC, LCDC

Copyright © 2023 Grace Communion International.
All rights reserved.
ISBN: **ISBN:** 9798390276754
Imprint: Independently published

GiANT Worldwide™, LP, and its assigns ("GiANT™") is the owner of, and reserves all rights in, certain intellectual property rights, including, but not limited to, the trademark "GiANT™", the trademark "GiANT Worldwide™", and copyrights in and to certain of the material included within the "GiANT Worldwide™ Toolkit" (2018 Edition) (collectively, the "GiANT™ Intellectual Property"). GiANT™ has licensed certain of the GiANT™ Intellectual Property to Grace Communion International for use in this book.

Forward

Greg and I are both well known for our "What if..." questions. I did a series of short "What if..." questions on Facebook a few years ago. "What if God DOES love you?" "What if you really ARE forgiven?" I also gave a series of "What if..." sermons when I was a pastor. The responses to both made me understand the value of questions and encouraging people to think through those questions. Facebook friends started sharing insights to their personal answers to the questions. Members started sharing how thinking through the questions helped them in their relationship with Father, Son and Spirit.

So when Greg asked me to edit the "What if Jesus..." book he and Mark wanted to write, I wanted to be involved. However, while I enjoy editing and working with these two men, I also knew it would be a challenge. Both men have a lot to offer, and both write well, but I wasn't sure they could write a book together. They are vastly different, and they look at things from very different perspectives. Greg writes, thinks, and speaks from the position of a teacher and leader of leaders; Mark writes, speaks, and thinks from the position of a pastor and counselor. Greg is visionary and focused on what the future could look like, and how can we get there. Mark focuses on people and how he can help them through their life journey – hopes, fears, challenges, trauma, and addictions. I love a challenge, so I said yes for three reasons.

One, I have known Greg for more than forty years, and we have worked closely together for the past decade. Mark and I became quite close the past four years. Two, I have learned to trust the Holy Spirit. I trusted that these two were supposed to write this book. And three, I knew both men were asking me to edit because they valued my input and ideas. I was being invited to participate in the planning and chapter ideas of the book.

Now that the book is done, I can share that it's been an inspiring journey. We struggled initially with both men writing from their different perspectives, and not knowing how to write from the other's point of view. It was like two books were being written. Both men felt strongly about how to approach the book, so we spent a weekend together to pray, share ideas, and listen to each other. We talked about the overall purpose of the book, what each of them wanted the reader to gain, what they believed the Holy Spirit was telling them to write. We talked about their passions and their different approaches. It was a joy watching the Holy Spirit inspire two men who have great respect and love for each other find ways to listen to each other's passions and work together to make this book what it is. Both men write from their strengths, their passions, and their professions. Greg writes as the leader of a denomination; Mark writes as a counselor, who is also a pastor.

Their primary goal was to answer the big question: What if Jesus is always with you – through the good, through the bad, and through the messy? What if it is true that he never leaves or forsakes us? What if he is there during all the pain, and anger, and loss, and hopelessness? What if he truly is the head of the church? The three of us decided to use the big question as the title of the book. Once we did this, we were able to develop the content a bit deeper. The formula we came up with for the book chapters enabled both men to use the gifts, talents, and experiences God has given them to make the book personal, inspiring, and hopeful. I enjoyed watching the passion for the book grow in both men.

I have to share from the outset that we are violating one of the primary rules of writing – know your audience. The original idea was the book would be written for students at our seminary, but Mark rightly pointed out that many church leaders don't go to seminary, and they need to know God is for them and with them. But why limit the book to one or more groups? We decided to trust the Holy Spirit to put this book in the hands of those who want to know Jesus deeper, to those who might need affirmation or encouragement, and to those who falsely believe Jesus just doesn't get what they are going through. So the book was written to emerging leaders, to the Grace Communion International church body that we serve and love, and to any and all who are hurting and lost. I guess that covers about everyone.

You have in your hands the final product. As much as I love Mark and Greg, I have to share that this book is written above and beyond both of them. We trusted the Holy Spirit through all the writing and editing, and as usual, we were amazed at the result. Not every chapter will speak as loudly to you – that's OK. Not every insight shared will reach your heart. That's OK too. Trust the Holy Spirit to lead you to the chapters that will bless you and trust him to lead others to the chapters that will bless them.

I pray you are as blessed reading this book as I was editing it. I pray you see that Jesus is the center of the center, that he is trustworthy because he is faithful, that he is always with you, and that you see him as your brother, your savior, your friend.

After all, what if Jesus is who he says he is?

Rick Shallenberger, Editor

Preface

Greg: Way back in 1981, when I was an undergrad college student, I took a racquetball class to fulfill an elective and because I love sports. There were eight students. We received basic instruction – this is a racquet, and you should keep the strap attached to your wrist for the safety of your opponent, these are the rules and off you go.

We began being matched to play one another in a round-robin fashion. My background in tennis helped me to become proficient quite quickly. I round-robined myself through my classmates until I met my nemesis. Mark Mounts was the one student who out-quicked me around the court and had the deadliest kill shot. There was no way to defend the shot that hit low on the wall and died immediately when it rebounded on the court.

Besides running me around the racquetball court, Mark was a great guy. I enjoyed his pleasant personality, his quick wit, and all-around good demeanor. Mark is the type of guy who can come across as anybody's best friend. You will come to know much more about Mark as the chapters unfold.

Fast forward to 2012. Both Mark and I had served in the pastoral ministry of Grace Communion International for more than twenty-five years. Unfortunately, we had assignments in different parts of the country and our lives seldom intersected. In June of 2012 we were both attending a regional conference in Dallas, TX. Before arriving, I was thinking to myself about reconnecting with Mark.

The opening night of the conference, I was in the basement of the Omni Hotel in the fitness center working out. Low and behold I ran into Mark and his wife Deb (this couple spends many dedicated hours lifting weights, climbing stair-like machines, stretching, and staying in top shape). After the sweating was over, we agreed to end our workout with a soak in the hot tub.

As we enjoyed the pulse of the jets on our fatigued muscles, we began catching up on the past twenty-five years. Talk of family and kids gave way to the professional experiences. Personally, I had been more involved in leadership at our denominational level and was connected to pastors across the country. Mark not as much. I asked Mark the fateful question that began a chain of events, all the way forward to the writing of this book – "How have you kept your head below the surface?" In other words, how has someone as talented and gifted as you remained almost anonymous? This was the "aha moment" for Mark to come out of anonymity and to become a strong voice for GCI's journey toward health (and ultimately a journey toward Jesus).

Mark: Today is February 10, 2022. Greg, Rick, and I have been working on this book for almost two years. I am in a hotel room in Charlotte, North Carolina preparing to give a presentation to pastors about how they need to set boundaries, maintain self-care, and know when a parishioner should be referred for counseling. I have been an ordained elder for almost thirty-five years. I have a master's degree, a license in Professional Counseling, and I am a Licensed Chemical Dependency/Addictions counselor. I just turned sixty-one this past December. My name is Mark Mounts; I'm the guy who beat the snot out of Greg on the racquetball court more than forty years ago.

When Greg asked me to co-author/collaborate on this book my initial response was "Sure." It's not the first time I've been asked to write a book.

I have been encouraged by church members, past and current therapy clients, peers with all sorts of letters behind their names, members of my recovery group (Al-Anon) and even my barber, to write a book about Debra's (my lovely wife of almost thirty-eight years) and my life, focusing on grace and integrating our spiritual journey and trials and what we learned numerous times over the past sixteen years. I never have started that book. Then Greg comes along and says, "we need to write this book." I say yes, but in the back of my mind I'm thinking, this is not the book that I'm supposed to write. So, allow me to take the time to explain why I'm partnering with Greg to write a book I never envisioned myself writing.

I became a pretty good racquetball player forty years ago because something deep inside of me has the need to do things very well. Most don't know that about me because I hide it very well. Let me tell you why. For most of the years of my life, I have been around the reality and chaos of addiction. You will read some of the details in this book. What I didn't know is that I had to become "something" in order to survive that experience. This was providentially revealed to me in the middle of my forty-eighth year. The irony is that revealing came as a result of someone very close to our family struggling with the disease of addiction. Being a long-time pastor and now therapist, I was going to help this person and keep them from going down the road that I had seen others travel. Little did I know that my mindset was actually the worst addiction of them all – codependence. I had no idea what that was.

My clinical training was initially in professional counseling, not addictions. And, I had never met anyone who had the guts to tell me I was codependent. In retrospect, my loving wife had tried for years, but to no avail. I just couldn't hear it (steps 10, 11 and 12 are alive and well in our marriage). So, one evening, I was attending a recovery meeting with the person I thought I could "save." During that meeting, a sober (seventeen years at that time, and still sober) crack addict came up to me and said, "You know something Mark, you're here to help that person get sober, but they aren't the worst addict; you are… and you need to get your __s into Al-Anon!" I complied, but I had no idea about the ups and downs of the road I was about to travel.

Everything I thought was right and true was shattered. No area was spared. It demolished my ideas about ministry, family, being a husband, a father, a therapist and a Christian; no stone was left unturned. I didn't start my step work for more than a year, and when I did, it took me more than two years to complete. I was so controlling that my sponsor had to approach me and tell me what I needed to do. Remember, I like to do things well and feel good about it. I won't do the risky stuff unless asked, but when I'm asked, I have to do it well. Looking back, it's clear I did those things in the hopes that an emptiness that was so deep inside of me might somehow be filled. I had no idea how manipulative and selfish I actually was.

So, do you see the paradox? I've been told I should write a book for the last sixteen years and never did! But, when asked to do so, in the context that I felt may be kind of risky and not what I thought should be done, I said "yes."

Greg's reason for writing this book is to share the story of how God works us through a "process of growth." He wants to share what he's learned as a leader and as our denomination's current president. He also wants to share how I've "coached" him along the way. We have been discussing the vision for this book for almost two years. Then, several months ago, Greg asked Rick to join us so that we could clarify the premise and come to a consensus on the book. Rick has been a blessing to both Greg and me by helping two men, who happen to have totally different ways of viewing the world and relating, sit down and work things out.

My personal and professional experience has shown me that deep down, we all have these fears and doubts in some way, no matter what situation we may be experiencing. And, if these feelings and thoughts are not considered in a manner that goes beyond "what do I do now…how do I fix this," they have the power to destroy our hearts, minds, and souls. And, even in the middle of what may feel like "hell" in that moment, God is intimately present and lovingly involved. So, the impetus behind this book is to hopefully help all those in leadership accept and understand that all of this "dealing with life" is a process, including for those in ministry. It's so much more than succeeding and failing, it's actually ALL relational.

That is essential to understand, because in my opinion, most full-time pastors, their spouse, and families are drowning right now. Some feel safe enough to admit this. During the recent COVID pandemic many pastors had to consider, and then possibly accept (they aren't the same), that the church as we have known it may never be the same. We had to remind ourselves that Jesus said he would build his church and the gates of "hell" (death) would not stop it. He wasn't surprised by the pandemic, and it will not stop his church from being built. It may, however, change the employment status of many pastors. I had prepared for this years ago.

I initially went to Graduate school to give myself an "out" if the full-time ministry didn't work for me. It was a tough time. We had previously adopted two children that are biological brother and sister, and they were now both in grade school. Finances were tight, stress was high, and frankly Deb and I didn't know if we could survive the stress of it all. There were also multiple personal health issues that will be referred to later. So, why didn't I leave pastoral ministry? Through all the ups and downs that Deb and I have been through, we both came to realize that the pain, doubt, and fear that we faced almost daily were possibly a road to something so deep, that we simply had to accept it as the means to reach the end of that road. I'm not saying we liked it; in fact, we hated it! Because, at the time, it simply didn't make sense. Even so, we both admitted that we loved the people we served. We knew they weren't ours, they belonged to God, but we loved them and we knew they loved us. So, we continued doing what we believed God wanted us to do.

We went through our own personal hell, but it was there we were able to truly accept how God was faithfully guiding us to where we are today. Through the years, I have seen miraculous spiritual enlightenment and life changing realizations when people are in the middle of a personal "hell." I tell a church leadership team it's OK when they face their personal "hell" because this is where God meets them and faithfully guides them in their ministry. This does not fit with most recent church growth models. But the truth is, many are already in their hell and don't know what to do. Many are afraid to state they have fears, or admit that they want to quit. Some are battling addictions, are in failing marriages, or have a teenager who attempted suicide last week and only they and the clinicians know. What if Jesus is with them in the midst of their hell?

This is why a man with a type "A" personality on steroids (that would be Greg, in my opinion), and an intuitive man who can patiently listen to people's "stuff for hours (while being aware of his need to control and manipulate), can agree on how to write a book. Both of us have had to personally go through what we will write about in this book. Both of us had to look at ourselves first, and then humbly listen to the other's point of view.

This has not been an easy process. And our hope is that by reading not only the content, but the process we had to go through to come up with the content, you will know you are not alone, and that truth will give you hope. Why? Because most Christians may actually be in hell right now, and not realize that they need to stop worrying about being there later. They need to take the risk to ask for help now – today. That is what Greg has done despite his personality. And ironically, he considers me his "helper," as I consider him mine in so many different ways that I never realized until I took the risk to say "yes" to his book proposal.

If Greg and I manage to pull off this book, you will know beyond a shadow of a doubt, that two professionally degreed old guys, who survived the transformation of their cultish religion to a spirituality and church based on grace and love, can hash things out despite their differences. And then you can begin to consider that in-spite of our profound personal differences, experiences and opinions, there is something deep inside the two of us that is beginning to accept that something greater than our experiences, our pain, our regrets and guilt, our vision, mission and goals, is now fueling our souls.

I think I can speak for the both of us in that we pray this book gives you hope. We pray this book helps you consider that in the middle of what may be your current hell, the light of heaven is shining. But it is a light that is different; it will feel and be risky. That is why grace and the perfect love of God in Father, Son and Spirit have profoundly offered to fill your soul with his presence, and to miraculously grace you with an awareness to know he's there. So, hold on, I think this is going to be quite a ride.

Table of Contents

Introduction 13

What if Jesus Truly is the Head of the Church?.................... 21

What if Jesus has Established His Church... 31

What if Jesus Knows You are Hurting...................................... 43

What if God's Grace is Sufficient?... 49

What if Longing and Yearning is God's Design for Us? 57

What if Jesus Knows the Reality of Life... 63

What if Jesus Really Understands the Human State (Us)... 69

What if Jesus' Love Really is Enough?..................................... 75

What if Jesus Understands our Fear, Anger and Depression? . 83

What if We Really Are Friends of Jesus.................................. 91

What if We Are Fully Known by Jesus?.................................103

What if Jesus Does Accept Us Just As We Are? 111

What if Jesus is Present With to the End of the Age?..................119

What if Jesus Really Does Provide Us with His Rest? 129

What if Jesus Really is the Head of the Church... and of Me?...133

What if Jesus...

Introduction

Greg: Why would we write this book? I think most pastors and church leaders would agree with me that it would be much easier to write volumes on what not to do in ministry, but not as easy to write on what works. With that said, most pastors and church leaders would also agree that learning to be a good pastor or church leader is a never-ending process. And there are good things worth sharing with others.

In the initial stages of thinking "Hey, I have some ideas I want to share, and I think it could be my second book," I had these two points in mind.

Continuation of providing high support and high challenge to our denomination's pastors in the most grace-filled way that we can (with the goals of better preparation, orientation, and overall care for our pastors).

This sounds good, reasonable, and worthy. After all, I am the President of Grace Communion International (GCI) and I take my role very seriously about the development and care of our pastors.

Once Mark realized I was genuine in wanting him to get more involved in GCI ministry training, he came to the Home Office to present a couple of sessions to our new pastors who were being oriented for their positions as field pastors. I asked Mark to help them understand the stark difference in pastoral counseling versus clinical counseling. Mark's presentations caused quite a stir, especially for a wide-eyed batch of fresh pastors, some of whom may have been on the edge of thinking they can play the role of savior to their awaiting congregations.

Mark's work with this fresh crop of pastors was enlightening and hugely helpful in saving them from a lot of potential unseen grief and rookie mistakes. It is within this vein of helping and equipping church leaders that Mark partnered with me, and his services have expanded beyond the orientation sessions.

And even though these are viable steps toward healthier pastors for healthier churches, this is not a strong enough reason for writing a book that is intended to be a gift to future leaders and required reading for a seminary class on church leadership. This leads me to my second point.

Offer a front row view into the journey of Grace Communion International with the sneaking suspicion that other churches and organizations may be wading through the same waters as us.

Rick Shallenberger, our editor, along with Dr. Tom Nebel, a partner of GiANT Worldwide™, and I co-wrote *A Giant Step Forward; Toward an Emerging Culture of Liberation*. This book provided an overview of Grace Communion International as I stepped into the presidency in October 2018 (GCI is a globally networked church with eight hundred churches in sixty-six countries). Dr. Nebel introduced us to an amazing tool called the Support Challenge Matrix. It was this tool that opened my eyes to the remarkable twists and turns that make up the history of our organization.

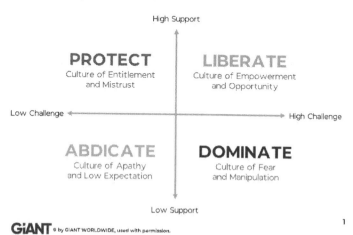

First, we had to admit that historically, we landed in the dominator quadrant with a strong focus on legalism. The movement away from legalism and domination started in the early '90s and got kicked squarely in the head during the mid-1990's. We had a short stop in the Abdicator quadrant as we dealt with our past and wondered about our future, eventually settling into the Protector Quadrant for almost twenty-five years.

Our second movement in the grace awakening of GCI was moving out of protectionism. Moving away from entitlement and mistrust was the challenge. This is the season I came into position of being the fourth President of GCI. To break out of a social club mentality, and perceived entitlement that had been linked to our Pasadena Headquarters, was uniquely ingrained with challenges. Each small step out of the Protector Quadrant has been a rich part of our learning with steady, incremental progress toward liberation.

Documenting our denomination's story of being transformed by grace has merit, however it still comes up short in what I believe I am to pass to our future leaders.

The "What if?" discussions I had with Mark sitting on his patio led us in the direction that we both felt passionate about and convicted to undertake. Instead of recounting (ad nauseam) what we have experienced and what we have learned, what if we talked about what we know to be true? Especially what we know to be real about the true Head of the Church?

I have accepted and come to own my calling to leadership as GCI President, and yet my highest calling is to follow Jesus. In turn, I echo the sentiment of the Apostle Paul when I ask those under my care to "Follow me as I follow Christ" (1 Corinthians 11:1). Leading through the supreme headship of Jesus as an under-shepherd is the only viable path before me. Framing leadership as leading with, like, and for Jesus in day-to-day participation is central to the overall contents of the book.

The Support Challenge Matrix helped us think beyond the cultural aspiration of liberation. The culture will never take shape without the Liberator, Jesus himself. It is the work of Jesus as the liberator in the individual lives of people and communities of people who form GCI. Formation can only happen in him.

For better or worse, my voice and my personal style of leadership will shape and influence the organization – so what I say and what I do is weighty during my season as president. I cannot simply preach Jesus to the church and then go about my private life pursuing personal ambitions and pleasures. To be a good leader, I must start by being a good follower – a follower of Jesus. It is a day-by-day existence of consciously connecting with my Lord. It is beginning each morning seeking his good and perfect will, followed by seeking his ongoing help throughout the day.

So, are Mark and I spiritual giants? We certainly don't think of ourselves in this way. As you read through the chapters you will read more about our warts, challenges, and shortcomings than about any spectacular victories. It is our hope that you see the strength of Jesus shining through our broken humanity.

You might notice we don't begin the book with what most might assume is the most fundamental "What if?" question: "What if Jesus really does love you and desires a personal relationship with you?" We are starting from the premise that you have already addressed this question in your life. As church leaders, Mark and I will start with what we believe to be the most important and fundamental question for pastors and ministry leaders – actually, for all Christ followers.

Mark's and my sole reason for writing this book – our specific purpose statement – <u>is to assure the reader of the centrality of Jesus</u>. We want to go beyond a "What's in it for me?" attitude. This book is about a deeper dive, more than seeing the personal benefits and blessings Jesus brings to humanity. We deeply desire that the reader comes away with a clarity about the depth of relationship that Jesus makes available to you and me, and all his children. The real and raw relationship of what Paul means when he says, "*I want to know Christ – yes, to know the power of his resurrection and participation in his sufferings, becoming like him in his death, and so, somehow, attaining to the resurrection from the dead*" (Philippians 3:10-11 NIV).

This Philippians passage is foundational for all we write. Embracing Jesus means coming to terms with our humanity in this fallen world, knowing and owning our shortcomings and limitations, and then really coming to know our utter dependence on him. Joining Jesus in his sufferings is only possible because he first joined our fallen world in flesh and blood and experienced all temptations known to man, yet without succumbing to sin. He gets us. We can look forward to attaining the resurrection to a glorified life only because Jesus has gone first. He has blazed the trail to bring many sons and daughters to glory.

Gaining Jesus and really knowing him is Mark's and my earnest desire for any person who takes the time to read through our chapters.

You have seen in Mark's and my comments in the preface that we are "wired and fired" quite differently. We view the contrasts in our personalities as a strength to the fabric of this book. The contrast of personality differences will hopefully create balance for the reader and a have a wider appeal to a broader audience.

Our editor noted that while I write more from the perspective of a survivor who is learning to live with Jesus as Lord and to thrive in this relationship, Mark is writing from a place of hope for victims who are in the discovery stage of learning about Jesus and his love (and who are we to argue with the editor). We encouraged Mark to write from his professional experience as a counselor, and as a pastor. It's a tall order, but our faith in him led to what you are about to read. Mark deals with people in pain and grief. We felt it important for Mark to show how Jesus is with us in our pain and grief, and one of the best ways to do that is to focus his chapters on the five stages of grief. This means his chapters will have a different flavor than my chapters, but both of us have the same goal – to show Jesus is always with us.

Throughout the book, you will note that Mark and I refer to GiANT Worldwide™ tools we've found quite helpful, as well as to different personality assessments we've taken over the years. I look at these assessments and tools as a method of learning how better to understand how God has wired me to serve him, and as a validation of the spiritual gifts he has given me. I know Mark feels the same way.

We hope you enjoy our adventures, and most of all, that in some personal, visceral, unique way, you are drawn closer to our Lord, Jesus.

We invite you to wrestle with the "Reflection Questions" at the end of most chapters. This is where it becomes personal and real for you.

Mark: This book is about stopping and giving yourself permission to consider that no matter what life is bringing your way in ministry and church work, Jesus is intimately involved in your work, and with you personally.

My chapters in this book will focus on my personal journey – as a husband, father, pastor, and counselor – through what we are actually writing about: the dynamics of change and the emotions one experiences as "deep change opportunities" are presented to us.

Two years ago, Greg asked me to do a two-day presentation with my idea of what it means for a human being to change. Uh, that's not complicated at all. But in Greg's classic manner, he made me think deeply about the assignment. As a result, I came up with a process of change that, in my opinion, generically includes four stages – knowledge, acceptance, experience and trust.

It goes something like this. You learn something new; you can accept it or not. If you don't, well…good luck with that one. If you do, the fun part we never consider begins. You will now experience your life from the perspective the new knowledge you have accepted gives you. And you might think it's going to be awesome. Hold on, because you also have to cope with the reality that not everyone will agree with the knowledge you've been "enlightened" with – let alone accept it in their personal context. And that is when all of us learn that trusting or not trusting will be the riskiest thing we ever do. I've experienced this in both pastoral ministry and professional counseling.

Have you ever considered what it means for a person to really change? I mean change at a heart, soul, and mind level. Think about it. Everything that you have thought, felt, and believed may have to be challenged. Why? Because if something needs to change, then those above-mentioned characteristics cannot stay the same. Do we think that is going to be a fun process? It's not. Truth be told, we as humans generally do not like change. So, with that in mind, I would like to propose that it is very possible that as a person truly, deeply changes, they will grieve the loss of their old thoughts, feelings, and beliefs. And this will be a deeply emotional experience…it's called grief.

That is why we have chosen to break this book down into the principles that are generally accepted with the five stages of grief. They are:

- Shock/Denial
- Anger
- Bargaining
- Depression
- Acceptance

We may not specifically mention the five stages by name, but our intention is to help church leaders and pastors understand that, in principle, it is normal to be emotional in the process of change and personal growth. It is also important to understand that these five stages are not fluid in the dynamic of change. One day you may have accepted something, only to be shocked to realize that you didn't understand a very important aspect of what you have just learned to accept. Life is an unpredictable process. You will hear me and Greg mention this quite a few times throughout the book.

So, with that in mind, my chapters will cover principles and experiences I have had from the knowledge, acceptance, experience, and trust aspects of change. You will also see that I have become quite familiar with the grief process we experience as change occurs. You can say, "I agree" to the chapters I write, or you can say, "I don't agree." Just remember, I believe your decision may be a part of your personal process. And, I don't say that frivolously. Your process may not automatically feel safer and more secure by the knowledge you may gain from what Greg and I write. So, once again, "What if Jesus…?"

What if Jesus...

Chapter 1 – Greg

What if Jesus Truly is the Head of the Church?

He himself is before all things, and in him all things hold together. He is the head of the body, the church; he is the beginning, the firstborn from the dead, so that he might come to have first place in everything. For in him all the fullness of God was pleased to dwell.
Colossians 1:17-19 NRSV

IT SEEMS APPROPRIATE that this first chapter would address what I consider one of the most important questions and set the tone for the ensuing chapters. So, let us begin the journey.

In October 2018, Dr. Joseph Tkach handed the presidential baton of Grace Communion International over to me. Does this somehow mean that I am now head of the denomination? The perception by some long-time members would frame my newly appointed office as sitting in a seat of church authority and making unilateral decisions on behalf of the denominational body. I knew in my spirit that this role was more about service than it was about being authoritative, and I was resolute that GCI was not going back to the

quadrant of domination. By the grace of Jesus, we came out of that slavery, and under the leadership of my dear friend Joe, we experienced what we call the "Grace Awakening" of GCI.

I have always known and continue to be reminded by the things I learn that Jesus is "The Head." My personal relationship to Jesus has been from childhood forward, and if you are like me, there are certain benchmarks along the way where I discover more and go deeper with Jesus. And so often it happens through my weaknesses. It is in my frailties and shortcomings that his strength is made great. The times when I have felt self-important and overly assertive, Jesus graciously brings a word of reason or correction to me (Mark has been the messenger from Jesus on several occasions).

During the prolonged season of the COVID-19 pandemic, our collective lives were disrupted. During the long summer months of 2020, while working from home and learning how to "zoom" all around the world, upon Mark's recommendation I immersed myself in reading Richard Rohr's book *Breathing Under Water*. This book challenged me to the core. How real, tangible, and vibrant is my relationship with Jesus? I did not feel beat up by the book, rather I felt inspired as I was drawn more closely to Jesus. In fact, I became even more convinced that as Jesus can be fully trusted to lead my life, he can likewise be fully trusted to lead his church (GCI being a small slice of the pie).

In many ways, my personal story is parallel to GCI's denominational story. Going back a little further, in 2016 we (GCI) began an intentional journey toward the quadrant of liberation – a culture of opportunity and empowerment. We began with what was called a "Core Group" — a group of nine men who committed to the process of self-discovery and self-disclosure through video conferences every two weeks for the course of a year. It was a commitment of time, but an even greater commitment of trust. You can read much more about this year in *A Giant Step Forward*, the book I wrote with our editor, Rick Shallenberger, and consultant, Tom Nebel.

The letting go of old baggage, and the collegial bonding that took place during that year was remarkable. Many of these original liberators went on to lead several other groups in the ensuing years.

Understanding that it takes common language to shape a culture, a critical development was allowing the GiANT™ language to permeate our organization and provide common terminology that has made teaching and learning much smoother. If concepts are not understandable and transferrable, then sustained change will not happen.

As a way of demonstrating some of the concepts and tools, here are a few helpful contributions we have incorporated from GiANT™:

Know Yourself to Lead Yourself

The fundamental concept of "knowing ourselves to lead ourselves" was a huge step forward in the journey toward liberation. To grasp what it is like for a person seated across the table to experience you is so helpful in clarity of communication and purpose, as well as healthy relationships.

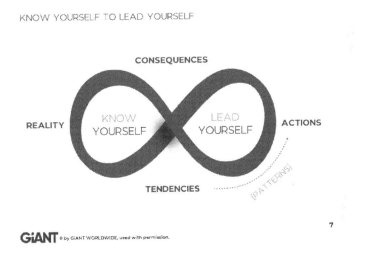

The Apprenticeship Square

The Apprentice Square (also called Developing Others) has been helpful in demonstrating the process of what it looks like for a seasoned person to walk with an unexperienced protégé into learning new skills. It reinforces our GCI value of "Life on Life" ministry.

What if Jesus...

APPRENTICESHIP SQUARE

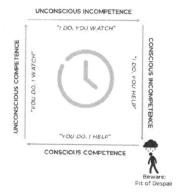

Five Voices

Identifying the voice order has helped our teams to be so much better at understanding one another and function more effectively. It helps individuals find their "best fit" on the team while elevating their respect for other voices.

Though Mark was not in that original group, his outside view of our work with the GiANT™ tools was insightful. He called it courageous because he saw that each of us displayed a willingness to open the door to greater honesty and vulnerability. However, it was just the beginning to opening the door to the transparency and authenticity we desire. He and I noticed this movement was and is nothing short of a major culture shift in our organization. As denominational leaders are allowed to explore the depths of their existence and move beyond codependent behaviors and personal insecurities to coming alive in Christ in a new, more robust way, the door then swings open for our pastors and ministry leaders. The critical question is, "How do we keep the door of liberation open for others, and how do we continue this movement down the hallway toward greater maturity?"

The following list of questions help us to examine and reflect on where we find ourselves in the journey forward.

- Do our leaders know themselves well enough to lead themselves and then be liberating leaders to others?
- Can each of us be defined by more than our foundational voices and personality traits?
- How are we prioritizing and managing our circles of influence?
- As mentors, what are we passing off to our apprentices?
- What signs of growth towards the culture of liberation and experience of GCI's fulfilled vision of Healthy Church are evident in this season?
- What transformation, breakthroughs, and collegial bonding is being experienced by leaders and ministry teams throughout GCI?
- In what ways are we acknowledging and living in the reality that Jesus truly is the Head of GCI?
- And most importantly, how are we yielding to Jesus as Lord and seeking his perfect will day by day?

Keep in mind that these questions are not just answered as "one and done." These are questions that must be considered with regularity if the church and its members are to maintain good health.

In December 2019, through colleagues in the National Association of Evangelicals, I was introduced to a book entitled "*The Fly in the Ointment.*" The author, J. Russell Crabtree, did incredible research and unearthed many factors that spoke to GCI's current position. There was a great deal of confirmation that much of what we were doing was on track. In fact, one of our leaders inquired if I had been following this book's guidance for a year or two in advance and was just now sharing. I can be a sneaky leader, but not this time.

The Fly in the Ointment pushes the envelope by challenging greater depth in leaders. For example, can a leader find satisfaction and fulfillment by investing in others behind the scenes and then rejoice in the success of the other? It takes a Christ-centered, spiritually mature person to fully invest in the other and allow them to be the one who gets the attention and accolades. To work out of a posture of "being for the other," it takes a leader who sees Jesus as Head of the church and to whom all glory is due.

The Fly in the Ointment specifically spoke to the role of ecclesiastical leaders at the regional level. The ones serving in the traditional role of "Bishop." These men and women are major influencers in that they have constant contact as direct supervisors. And as supervisors, they serve as a mashed-up mix of trainer, consultant, coach, counselor, boss, encourager, co-worker, and friend. But most of all they must be a Christ-follower exuding Christ-like responses. In GCI these ecclesiastical leaders are called Regional Directors (RDs).

When RDs are healthy and operating well, they are like the ligaments and tendons that connect muscle to bone and allow the body to function as it was designed. Ligaments and tendons are connective tissues holding the body in place, and so is the function of the Regional Director working with and through the pastors pointing them first and foremost to Jesus the Head of the church and then helping them to stay in alignment with Christ's body on earth – the church.

Beyond the important connective role of a Regional Director, it is our hope that they also will be like Paul was to the Corinthian church when he invited them to follow or imitate him as he reflected the nature, purpose, and love of Jesus. We are asking for more than diligent oversight and administrative efficiency from our RDs. We are asking them to function with Jesus as Lord of their lives, and then to constantly point others to him. This is the progressive journey from the open door of liberation down the hallway toward spiritual maturity.

The Apostle Paul used a curious word only found in his letter to Philippi— "Yokefellow"—that speaks with greater clarity to the role Christian leaders serve to their junior partners. The intent of yokefellow is beyond being a companion or friend; it is serving as a partner, working shoulder-to-shoulder pulling together in the same direction. It is a bonded relationship of shared values, vison and goals that find expression in laboring together, rejoicing together, and suffering together.

The depth of a yokefellow relationship requires intentionality, a commitment of focus and time, genuine love, and care. This deeply knitted relationship can only be experienced with a rather tight circle as it requires accumulation of shared experiences over months, years, and decades. In our human condition we have limitations of time, distance, and capacity, so therein lies the challenge. But within that challenge there is always opportunity to be seized. Moving from supervisor to yokefellow is not easy, it will take constant attention and intentional action. By the power of the Holy Spirit, it can be accomplished.

For our current Regional Directors, we have seen how they have developed genuine yokefellow relationships with one another. The quality of their shared work has made positive differences in GCI. As we celebrate these relationships, we now focus on passing along what has been received to other faithful men and women. And we trust that over time this same level, quality and texture of relationship and leadership will get passed from pastors to ministry leaders, and ministry leaders to ministry workers.

This depth of care and relational bond is the quest before us. However, this may be one piece of a bigger puzzle. In a recent reading of Jon Ritner's book, *Positively Irritating*, my thinking was challenged. What if we are building on what we already know and what has gone before? What if the familiar way of thinking and doing is holding us back from where the Spirit may be seeking to transform?

A big "What if?" for GCI is, "What if we are teaching out of book knowledge and simply passing on good information?" Can information bring about the innovation and transformation we so earnestly desire? In chapter 2, I will talk more in depth about the power of imitation, and how it takes the combination of information and imitation to bring about traction toward innovation.

The Spirit has been awakening us to see how some of our leaders are excellent relational leaders with the needed administrative skills, and then there are others who are emerging as good, on-the-ground ministry practitioners. Historically, we have readily admitted that there are no omnicompetent leaders, and yet somehow, we still are hopeful that these "Swiss Army Knife" kind of leaders are among us. Call it cognitive dissonance. And we are back to the foundation of this chapter, only Jesus himself is omnicompetent.

So how do we journey ahead?

Moving Forward

The body can only move and act as the head sends signals. As a teenaged athlete I learned in a raw, physical way that where the head moves, the body follows. This was handy information to play the position of linebacker in American football.

It is only through a positive response to Jesus, the Head of the church, that we will journey forward.

Let's return to the opening passage from Colossians chapter one. What do we learn about Jesus? He is before all things – before time and the material world existed. He is the creator who brought all we see and know into existence. Eugene Peterson in The Message Bible says *"everything got started in him and finds its purpose in him."*

This means Jesus is the creator and conserver of the known universe. And more than a God of the cosmos, he is personally, intimately involved with his creation. He so loved his created fallen children that he became flesh and blood to save them and lead the regeneration by being firstborn from the dead. Likewise, when it comes to the church, it is Jesus who organizes it and holds it together.

Jesus is faithful and always holds to his place as Head of the Church. The big question is how do we respond to him? In GCI, we speak about joining with Jesus using the term "Divine Participation." What we mean by this is that as we become aware of God's incredible grace towards us through Jesus Christ, and we realize he has invited us to participate in his good work, we respond by joining Jesus in what he is presently doing in our world. We respond to the Lord's amazing gift of salvation and relationship by participating with him through spiritual practices of worship and witness.

In its *worship,* the church gathers around Jesus, the center of the center. This happens in an individual's life through private prayer, Bible study, meditation and learning to relate to the relational Triune God. This also happens in corporate worship through meetings involving fellowship with other believers, public scripture reading, songs of worship, preaching, communion, group discussions and the like.

In its *witness,* the church flows outwardly to the world. In an article titled, *The Church and its Ministry*, Dr. Gary Deddo says this:

"The book of Acts gives us a clear vision of the sending of the church as witnesses to Christ in the world. At the beginning of the book, as Jesus prepares his followers to receive his Holy Spirit in a new and deeper way, he says this: 'You shall be my witnesses, in Jerusalem, Judea, Samaria, and to the uttermost parts of the earth.' Notice the progression from the city they are in, Jerusalem, to the most immediate surrounding area, Judea, to a more distant and culturally and religiously different area, Samaria, and finally to the most distant lands—the uttermost parts of the earth (Acts 1:8). In all these places there is one goal: be witnesses (pointers) to Jesus Christ as his representatives."

"Pointers to Jesus Christ" is who we are. As followers of Jesus our privilege is to participate in his ongoing ministry under his Headship. Participation is on his terms, not our own—a participation that is with Jesus (he never leaves or forsakes us), like Jesus (never breaking a bruised reed), and for Jesus (all glory and honor belongs to him).

Conclusion

I already mentioned the impact of *A Fly in the Ointment* as a book that informs the challenges of our church leadership and its relational dynamics. So, I will often speak out of a corporate voice on behalf of GCI. Mark will cite other sources that have helped him through his personal journey of healing and coming to know Jesus more and more. He will speak more directly to the experiences and responsibilities of the individual.

In short, our book is about seeing and submitting to Jesus as "first priority" in all matters. Jesus remains the Head even when we allow other objects, pursuits, or relationships to be temporary idols.

I have heard many believers say the phrase: "Let's make Jesus the center," or "Let's put Jesus in the center." I'm sorry you cannot do it, nor do you have to. Jesus IS the center, the unmovable center. Continually, patiently pursuing us. He never moves away from us, always toward us. Let that sink in.

So, the journey continues. How can this marvelous picture of healthy church with deep relationships, impactful mentoring, and fruit-bearing ministry happen? How does it get passed on to others? Only when Jesus is rightly recognized in first place in all relationships and endeavors. We start with Jesus, then we invite others to follow as we follow Jesus.

Reflection Questions

- How does the concept "Jesus is the creator and conserver of the known universe" resonate with you?
- The Bible is crystal clear about the primacy of Jesus as head over the church. If this in fact true, what are the implications?
- What are your thoughts and feelings about GCI's reflective evaluation as to how they collectively respond to Jesus as head of the church?

Chapter 2 – Greg

What if Jesus has Established His Church...

...and clearly set offices of leadership for the purpose of establishing faith in and relationship with himself?

The gifts he gave were that some would be apostles, some prophets, some evangelists, some pastors and teachers, to equip the saints for the work of ministry, for building up the body of Christ, until all of us come to the unity of the faith and of the knowledge of the Son of God, to maturity, to the measure of the full stature of Christ.
Ephesians 4:11-13 NRSVA

I CAME ACROSS AN INTRIGUING QUOTE that says, "When the student is ready the teacher will appear" (unknown origin).

As a pioneer, I am all about good organizational structures and systems supported by good ministry tools and practices (I could talk for hours about GCI's structure and polity). However, no matter how sound the organizational model, we cannot accomplish what we hope for unless we start with a spirit of humility and teachability. As the wise saying suggests, there needs to be "readiness" within the spirit of our would-be leaders.

We define readiness as a stage when a person displays the willingness and capacity to receive instruction, and then engages and acts in fresh, Christ-like ways. We find both spirits of teachability and engagement evident in the great story of Philip and the Ethiopian eunuch.

On the heels of the martyrdom of Stephen in the early church, followers of Christ scattered from Jerusalem to avoid persecution. Philip "the evangelist" was one of those followers. (He was one of the original seven deacons described in Acts 6.)

Philip was directed by an angel of God (Acts 8:26) to go to Gaza, where he would encounter a eunuch from the court of the queen of Ethiopia in Africa. (This eunuch was apparently either following or at least exploring Judaism). The eunuch was returning from a pilgrimage to Jerusalem, traveling south to his home country, Ethiopia.

The eunuch was reading from the writings of the prophet Isaiah—specifically a passage about the suffering of the promised Messiah. The eunuch did not know how to interpret what he was reading. He was a ready and willing student in need of a teacher. Philip, the able teacher and preacher, explained to him how the prophecy had been fulfilled by the life, death, and resurrection of Jesus, who was the Messiah talked about in the ancient writings. Philip shared the Gospel!

As they rode together in the eunuch's chariot, they came upon a body of water, and in response to the gospel, the eunuch professed his faith in Christ, and requested Philip to baptize him. Philip obliged, and then was immediately carried away by the Holy Spirit to another location. The eunuch continued homeward rejoicing in the salvation and new life that he had received in Jesus.

This account in the book of Acts leaves us hanging regarding the rest of the eunuch's story. It is reasonable to infer that the eunuch would have been the first to bring and share the gospel message to Ethiopia and the continent of Africa—thus, fulfilling Christ's proclamation in Acts 1:8 for the spreading of the gospel from Jerusalem, Judea, Samaria, and to the ends of the world. A really big deal.

Why the eunuch? Why this marvelous encounter with Philip? Undoubtedly, a divine appointment was at play — the angel instructing Philip to pursue the eunuch, the interaction with the scriptures and its fulfilled meaning in Jesus. The regeneration symbolized and experienced in the act of baptism. Then the Spirit redirecting Philip onto his next excursion. Movement, action, and change flowing out of the aspect of "readiness."

For the eunuch, he was finally seeing something clearly for the first time, even though it had always been there; the Old Testament puzzle pieces had finally been joined to display the magnificent picture that is Jesus Christ, the promised Messiah. The light came on and changed his life forever. The teacher (the faithful minister) appeared when the student was ready.

This Bible story is about this state of readiness. When I say "readiness," the posture of the eunuch is a great illustration. He was open and teachable with a desire to learn. When the light came on about Jesus being the fulfillment of the prophecies, he embraced the truth and displayed his surrender and allegiance through the act of baptism.

In Paul's correspondence to the church at Ephesus (cited above), he explains why we have teachers in the church like Philip the evangelist. Paul wants all believers to come to the same understanding about Jesus that the eunuch displayed. It is crucial for the community of the church to have a thorough and unified knowledge, and subsequent teachings of Jesus, and then to live out this unified faith. But get this, the journey of faith is a process of maturity—growth and movement away from childish behavior and toward Christlikeness. In other words, toward a life overflowing with love, joy, peace, patience, kindness, generosity, faithfulness, gentleness, and self-control (Galatians 5:22-23). A life that looks like and represents Jesus, who lives in us through the Spirit.

Readiness is embracing this growth process with the assurance that the Holy Spirit is continuing a good work in us, moving us closer to and making us more like Jesus. This is not a clever behavioral modification program, but rather a dynamic work of the Spirit. Please understand that the Spirit is constantly at work, not just showing up in times of crisis and only working part-time hours. The Spirit is always in you and always available to do a good work in you.

My good friend and one of GCI's Regional Directors, Anthony Mullins, gave me permission to share this story with you to emphasize the meaning I am trying to convey. Anthony, who serves as RD, local church pastor, and moderator of a GCI podcast (Gospel Reverb), came to me and confessed that he was in a dry season and felt devoid of joy. This emptiness was becoming spiritually paralyzing. Instead of enumerating the multiple circumstances and situations in his busy life that may be obstacles blocking the joy, he simply wanted me to join him in prayer to entreat the Holy Spirit to freely restore the spiritual fruit of joy to his life.

Please understand that Anthony had an open posture to discussing his life circumstances and challenges, and was quite honest about areas that needed attention and fresh responses from him. However, the inner joy that abides in a believer regardless of the ups and downs was not going to come by fixing a schedule, or much worse, trying to fix other people or himself. This was not a behavioral-modification problem, rather a circumstance that only the Spirit could change. Anthony's posture of humility and submission to and reliance on the Spirit was the game-changer. Anthony was declaring that he needed super-natural fixing that could only happen through the power of the Holy Spirit acting in his life. This is what we prayed for and the Spirit was more than able to fulfill.

I also see a kinship with Anthony and Philip in how they join Jesus in his ministry. They are both servants who are fully sold out for Jesus, going about their days freely sharing the good news about the Savior, and are open and receptive to the lead of the Spirit with an ever-forward trajectory of growth toward the stature and fullness of Jesus. Always pointing to Jesus and sensitive to the guidance of the Spirit. Always growing. Always sharing. Always about Jesus.

Coaching Triangle

Information

Learning how to be pastoral in the ways that we see Philip and Anthony is more of an art than a science. Yet picking up the skills and especially the spiritual intuitiveness doesn't happen accidentally. It begins with clear, biblical training about the role of a pastor. It begins with good information. We are so committed to the good information which includes Incar-national Trinitarian Theology and sound Biblical interpretation that we support and operate an online seminary – Grace Communion Seminary.

The Coaching Triangle that GiANT Worldwide™ allowed us to use in our GCI Toolkit shows that the byproduct of information and imitation is innovation. Innovation, meaning more than a "new widget." It is taking sound teaching and healthy practices and adapting them to your setting, your generation and your culture.

The combination of sound, biblical truth with the "life-on-life" experience of learning from veteran church leaders not only brings innovation to our fellowship, it brings transformation and regeneration.

COACHING TRIANGLE

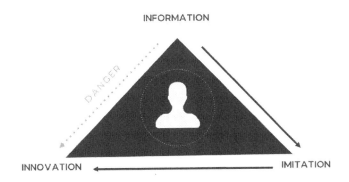

GiANT © by GiANT WORLDWIDE, used with permission.

4

Having this process to be a normal, habitual way of operating in GCI could possibly be the biggest game-changer we have been hoping for.

In GCI we train and coach our pastors to follow the New Testament instruction of Paul and we describe this with the 4 E's – Engage, Equip, Empower, and Encourage. We feel so strongly about these principles that we use the 4 E's for the framework of our pastoral job description in our formal Human Relations file of GCI.

By engage we mean that a pastor creates and fosters an environment of recruitment and invitation. This is not an executive head-hunting business, rather it is a careful practice of seeing people. Seeing people for how they are wired, what skills they display and where their passions lie. Then inviting them into participation within the community and ministries of the church. Calling them into what the Spirit has been shaping them for.

Equipping involves exposure to new opportunities with the goal of developing new skills. Most importantly, equipping happens through mentoring relationships. In all aspects of our ministries, from the pastor to ministry team leaders, to the lead technical operator, to the door greeters and coffee servers, we expect that all have someone under their wing that they are training and passing along their skills and knowledge. We always want avenues where others may learn and join in. We like to say, "Never do ministry alone, always include someone else." This component of imitation is how ministry values, styles and skills are caught.

I have emphasized the practical application of learning, which is highly relational and somewhat informal, and yet the formal side of equipping is equally important. We believe good pastoral ministry is both "taught and caught" (our Coaching Triangle shows the need for good information and good imitation). We provide sound biblical training and theological foundations through our institutes of higher

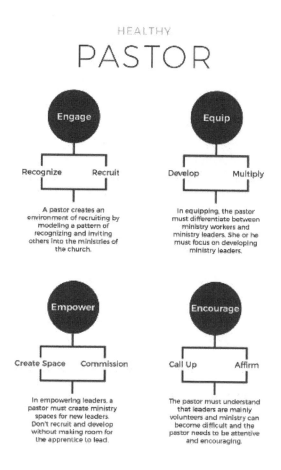

learning and supplement these with conferences, workshops and a monthly periodical aptly called "The Equipper."

Empowerment is tricky because there are risks. To empower is to hand over meaningful responsibility to another. What if they don't do it like I do? What if they make mistakes? The short answer to these two questions is, it's okay. An empowered person will do it their way, maybe even better. An empowered person will make some mistakes as they learn and develop. Who hasn't made mistakes? And maybe the hardest lesson in empowerment is experienced by the veteran leader who, out of a spirit of humility, must decrease so the other can increase. John the Baptist understood this and applied it (John 3:30).

Encouragement is the fun part. It's where the veterans get to observe and offer words of affirmation to the newly emerged leaders. It's akin to a parent celebrating their child's first steps or solo bike ride. This is where the veteran leader needs to remember that their attention is needed, and their affirming words are like apples of gold in pictures of silver. One of my greatest heartaches in over years of ministry has been when I have been elevated in position and responsibility and I am not certain that my predecessor is still mindful of what I am up to. The noticeable lack of attention can be even more stinging than the harsh words of criticism. I must be mindful and intentional to be an encourager myself.

For any of our senior leaders, never underestimate how powerful your words of encouragement are for the generation coming behind you. One of our kindest and most loved retired leaders is a gentleman named Carn Catherwood. In my first year of being President and stumbling along trying to learn my role and how to best serve the good people of GCI, I was at a pastor's conference in Dallas, TX. After the meeting, Carn made his way forward to intercept me and offer the most assuring words: *"Greg, you are God's man for the church at this time."* Those words, like a strong tailwind, have carried me for quite some time. Thank you, Carn, for being an encourager at a crucial time for me.

Imitation

Having a clear, spelled out under-standing of pastoral ministry is a great start, but like all disciplines there must be practice, and it is especially better when a seasoned veteran can walk the eager protégé around the apprentice square.

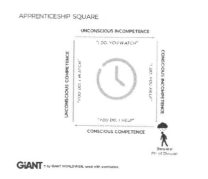

The mentoring I speak of is a deep imitation of a minister who has gone before. It is the protégé who follows Paul, as he follows Jesus. It is the qualified understudy to whom Paul has passed along the truly meaningful things he has gained from knowing Jesus and from having served the church for decades. This level of learning takes commitment from both sides, the teacher and the pupil. And it takes time. Think of the concept of ten thousand hours (equivalent to ten years of work) necessary to become an "expert." The development of good godly leaders happens in relationship and over large chunks of time. It cannot be rushed. GCI and the greater Christian church need to be more committed to the Pauline practice of mentoring.

Adding another layer, consider that Paul identifies his investment in others as that of a "spiritual father" to spiritual sons and daughters. In 1 Corinthians 4:16 Paul says to imitate him, and yet he has a dilemma. Paul is deeply involved with the Ephesian church and cannot return to them at this juncture. His solution is to pen a letter and to send his "spiritual son," Timothy, who is faithfully imitating Paul, representing his "ways in Jesus." Timothy was ripe for the assignment. In a life-on-life, patient, methodical, intentional, fatherly fashion, Paul invested in Timothy and others. This is how Christ-like leaders are developed.

It is striking to read in the body of Paul's letters that he doesn't posture his mentoring relationships as teacher to disciple, rather he uses familial language – father to son. It speaks to the depth of care, closeness and even long-term desire for the protégé.

I have been extremely fortunate to have been given several different "Paul" figures in my life. I could speak about a couple of pastors who poured into my life early on as I was a trainee and assistant in ministry. Their deposits were deep and foundational, and I am eternally grateful. I think it is more important that I share examples of relationships that were crucial as I was being called to higher levels of opportunity and greater roles of service. This can be a good addition to the earlier stories of the eunuch's call to salvation in Jesus and Anthony's call to the sanctifying work of the Holy Spirit.

As I look back over the past fifteen years of my life, I recognize three occasions where men played the role of the Apostle Paul in my life. In the spring of 2006, I received a call of invitation from Dr. Richard Wynn. In the spring of 2011, I was asked a curious question by Dr. Dan Rogers. Then in the spring of 2014, I was challenged by Dr. Joseph Tkach. I suppose I should be alert to the spring seasons in my life, and especially when doctors of Christian ministry invite, question, and challenge me.

In 2006, I was working in a dual career role in Fayetteville, NC – pastoring a GCI congregation and serving as Executive Director of a Youth for Christ (YFC) chapter. Susan and I were in the early stages of having a new house constructed (we owned the lot, had a floor plan and were in negotiation with a contractor). This was the timing for Dick Wynn to phone from out of the blue. He was the Board Chairperson for Metro Atlanta YFC.

Dick was the former President of YFC and was one of the influential trainers in my association with them. He called to invite me to come to Atlanta and oversee one of the larger chapters in the YFC organization. Even more attractive was the opportunity to be under his oversight and mentorship. This would mean not only dissolving our home construction plans, but we had to face the greater challenge of stepping away from pastoral ministry. Wait, in the culture of GCI, pastors only step aside if they are of retirement age, or they die while in office. What was I considering?

Sorting out this invitation was no small thing. It was Susan who encouraged me to accept the invitation and to travel to Atlanta for the interviews with YFC Board and staff. Through the long process of prayer, discussion and "all things considered," we accepted the position with Metro Atlanta YFC and moved. The deposits of Dr. Wynn into my life were huge. I can sum up his aspiration for me in the statement, "Greg, we want you to be a leader of leaders." It was to this end that Dick trained, coached, and mentored me.

In 2011, I was again in a dual career role – the result of the financial crisis of 2008/09 – Executive Director YFC and now Generations Ministries Coordinator for GCI. That spring, Dr. Dan Rogers asked me, "Greg, can you go back to school and get a doctorate?" I thought I had said good-bye to school when I achieved my Master of Arts degree in Christian Ministry. I wasn't necessarily intimidated by more schooling, but why and for what purpose? Then Dan explained further, "I think you can do my job." Oh!

I think of my relationship with Dan in various stages. My early experience was admiration as a young man who gleaned a lot from Dan's teaching, and especially his gift for inspirational preaching. He made God real and approachable. The second stage was working for Dan. I would say "alongside." Dan always gave me great latitude to create and experiment with new approaches. His trust was a huge kindness to me. And now that I am President of GCI, Dan and I share a collegial type of friendship that is tricky to explain. We talk more openly and candid, we lament and laugh, and we are in awe of what God has done in GCI. A good space.

In the spring of 2014, I found myself sitting alongside Dr. Joseph Tkach in the booth of "Club Route 66" and I recall we were eating a special pistachio-encrusted salmon plate in a miso sauce that only this restaurant served. My good friend Joe is what we would call a "foodie," and he is deeply convicted that sharing a meal with another person is one of the most spiritual experiences one can have (and I agree). On this occasion, it wasn't entirely about bonding and deepening friendship; it was what I call "challenge time."

The time had come for me to step into Dan Roger's role as Director of US ministries for GCI, and it was Joe's place to confirm the transition. Over a lovely meal and fancy cocktail, Joe looked me square in the eyes and said, "Greg, we need you to move to Glendora and operate out of the national office." But Joe, Susan and I are comfortable in our NC mountain home, and our extended family is close by. Greg, how will you develop the working relationships you must develop and help shape the office you will one day oversee? But Joe, I can come out for a week or two at a time and allow Susan to remain happily stationed in her routine with the life we have made there. Greg, we need Susan to be a part of this transition too. The staff needs to interact with you as a couple, and plus, I really like Susan and her demeanor. Joe, you make a good case.

In hindsight, as difficult as it was to say farewell to our family on the east coast, the move to California and living there for four years was absolutely necessary. The proximity to Joe and his willingness to make himself available to me was invaluable The bonding with staff proved to be crucial as we prepared to make the major move from Glendora to Charlotte, NC in 2018. Further, the fact that Susan and I moved first was vital as each member of the Glendora staff had to choose whether to move across country or not.

Dick, Dan, and Joe are godly men whom I admired and respected mostly because of how they faithfully and sacrificially served Jesus and his church through all kinds of circumstances. For me, Jesus spoke into my life through their invitations, questions, and challenges. Apparently, each of these men saw something in me that I didn't fully recognize. Their promptings and personal deposits in my life have shaped and guided a course for what Jesus has had in mind for my life – in other words, his calling on my life. Hindsight enables me to see his hand in everything. He is the one who prepared me and placed me where I am today. My prayer is every leader sees his hand in their life.

Conclusion

For all the engaging, equipping, empowering, and encouraging we can offer, it can only work when there is also the underlying spirit of humility, the mindset of readiness, and the acknowledgement that Jesus is involved and always in charge. The willingness and availability of Philip, grouped with the teachability and responsiveness of the eunuch, provides us with a beautiful conversion story of someone who is "far off" coming to Jesus. The complimentary story of Anthony amplifies the vulnerability and deep reliance on the power of the Spirit to produce the rich fruit of the Spirit into our lives. Then my personal story with all the twists and turns in my life – guided by what I like to call "the ministry rock climbers ahead" who have pioneered a true path – shows the importance of reaching back to bring another along. It was "readiness" that began the movement in all these stories.

Together these stories show us the journey of calling, maturation, and the deep relationship into which our Lord has called us and is taking us. As Head of the Church, Jesus has been faithful to continually raise up church fathers and mothers through the ages, who then pass along the things that they have learned from a life with Jesus to other qualified, willing men and women who continue the life and fabric of the church.

What a ride we are on to grow in grace, knowledge, and relationship with Jesus the Head of the Church. We do this individually in our devotional life with Christ, AND we do this in community with other believers. We are created for relationship, not isolation. The beauty of what the Lord has established is to give you and me space where we find belonging and purpose embedded in relationship to him and within the corporate context of his body, the church. Are you ready?

Reflection Questions

- How do you view the church? What is the need for offices and people who have gone before us?
- What are the dynamics of calling? We stressed a posture of "readiness," but what are other important factors? In what ways do you see the components of challenge, change, sacrifice, relationship? What others?
- What does Jesus have in mind for your life at this stage? What about the future?
- Who has he placed in your path to invite, question and challenge you?
- What is your state of readiness? How teachable and ready to engage are you?

Chapter 3 – Mark

What if Jesus Knows You are Hurting...

...and that pain is a part of the process of healing?

My brothers and sisters, whenever you face trials of any kind, consider it nothing but joy, because you know that the testing of your faith produces endurance; and let endurance have its full effect, so that you may be mature and complete, lacking in nothing.
James 1:2-4 NRSVA

AS I MENTIONED IN THE INTRODUCTION, I am going to take a different approach to the "What If?" questions than Greg is taking. As our editor mentioned, and Greg quoted in the introduction, Greg is approaching these topics from a survivor point of view. He is able to put the past behind him and continually focus on the hope we have in Jesus, always acknowledging that Jesus is the center of the center. I appreciate his approach – that's Greg. I deal with hurting people on a daily basis, including pastors and ministry leaders. My approach will come from my educational experience, helping lead you from hurt to healing – all of which includes Jesus. We both focus on the centrality of Jesus, but we do so from our different personalities and approaches.

Many years ago, when I found the courage to first attend an Al-Anon meeting (12-step program for family members of addicts and alcoholics), I was met by a wonderful woman who had been through absolute hell. At the end of the meeting, she came up to me, looked me straight in the eyes and said two things. "Mark, you are exactly where you are supposed to be" (we'll talk about that one later in the book).

And then she said, "If your process goes the way that will really help you, you are going to grieve." Grieve? What in the world did she mean? Well, I was about to find out.

Before we get into what grief means, I would like to "give you" two phrases. The first is:

"You don't know, and you don't know that you don't know."

Here's the second:

"Your response to a 'crisis' is more important than the 'crisis' itself."

As Greg and I write more about the idea of Jesus being the Head of the church, I encourage you to remember these two phrases. Why? Well, the first one is another way of saying that "grace" is upon you. The second one helps you consider that when you realize that "you didn't know," and "you didn't know that you didn't know," your response to that reality will be just as important, if not more important, then what you now know or have learned.

The principles that Greg is sharing in these chapters may seem very reasonable and even "Godly". Yes, they are "Godly", and you would agree with that until you encounter something that you think you can control and "fix", only to find out you had absolutely no idea what was going on, let alone having the ability to "fix it." When this happens – and it's not "if", it's "when" – the two phrases above will become more and more relevant; at least I hope they do.

When I counsel or coach pastors, every one of them has come to me with the intention of "becoming a better pastor for God and for the church." This sounds good and extremely convicted. My response to them is, "Have you ever considered that God technically doesn't need you?" After they recover from their shock, I explain it this way: God doesn't need any of us, but he does want us. In other words, God is just fine on his own, thank you very much, but he loves when we participate with him, when we join him in what he is doing. So why ministry? Why the church? The simple answer is because he loves us unconditionally – grace. Even so, that does not mean that all will respond to the grace of God in the same way. If you think they will, you have just run head on into the two phrases that I wrote about earlier.

Have you ever considered what needs to occur for a human being to change? Let's talk about Pastor A. First, she must consider that change is necessary and possible. But why would she consider that? Well, maybe it's because something isn't working out the way she thought, or maybe she heard something new that she had never considered before. Great, so she decides to "change." And when she does, the systemic effect of that change will be unavoidable. And we pray the "system" adjusts accordingly.

Let me explain. Let's say Pastor A wants to be more organized. First, she starts contacting her ministry leaders once a week. This seems reasonable. But then, she begins to get comments like, "this is too much," or "you don't need to call me that often, I've got it under control." Or she could hear, "well it's about time…I'm drowning over here…I thought you didn't care!" So, she's a little surprised to say the least, maybe even shocked. She didn't know…oops. Now, she starts to get defensive, tries to convince others she does care, or she "sticks her nose in" where it may not be wanted because some of her leaders want to do things their way, not the way this "pastor" thinks they should be done.

We all think we want change, but what we may really want is for things to go our way, calmly. That's where the idea of Jesus being in charge, not you, opens the door for that grief I mentioned earlier. What do I mean? You're not always going to get your way. You're not going to be understood all the time. You're not going to be liked by everybody, and you still may have to work with them. You may not be able to change much of anything or anybody. But you didn't know, and you didn't know that you didn't know.

Think of it. If you truly believe that Jesus oversees the church, that statement dogmatically says that you are not in charge…period. Do you really want to change that reality? I don't. Why? We know what it looks like when we believe we are in charge. History shows us. When Jesus came to offer us a way of life that would change our entire way of thinking, feeling, and behaving – a way of life that would give us life eternal – we tortured him and hung him on a cross to die!

So, what will bring on the grief? The reality that you can't change anybody. Once you accept the truth that everybody sins and you can't change them, you realize that you have to learn to cope with people in the midst of their sins, just like everybody else. And that, my friends, can feel like you are dying on the inside…which we will see is what Jesus said it would be.

So, what is grief and how do you move from hurting to healing? For the sake of this book, we will use the "5 stage" model. I know there are other models, but we don't want this book to be seven hundred pages, and I don't think you do either. So, here they are.

Stage One: Shock/Denial

Yes, it's really that simple. It's when you are in the middle of an experience, and you simply can't believe it's happening or has occurred. At times it feels like a dream, or unreal. This is what we experience when a loved one dies. This is what your members will experience when one of their family members commits suicide, or has an affair with another church member, or "comes out of the closet," or overdoses on drugs, or becomes a victim of a "drive-by" two days after they've received a scholarship to an Ivy League University. You may say, "Mark, that will never happen while I'm the pastor of this church." My answer is, "I'll pray for you." These are situations that cannot be fixed, and we must learn to cope with them. And to cope with them, you first must get over your own personal shock that as a pastor or ministerial leader, you will find yourself in the middle of these experiences.

Stage Two and Three: Depression and Anger

You may think, I'm never going to get depressed. OK, but you may get very angry. And if you don't learn to admit that you're angry, (oops...that's change), chances are you will eventually get depressed. Why? Because unresolved anger takes its toll on you. Anger is a part of the fight, flight or freeze response. And a person can be in this state most of the time and not even know it (there are those sayings again...darn). And this angry state will eventually change your brain chemistry, and you will more than likely experience depression. The problem is, the anger state may be what you would consider your "normal." But you don't know that (need I say it...). So, when you are told that you may need help, that people are now worried about you, or you just don't seem yourself lately (denial), you just get more angry or more depressed.

Stage Four: Acceptance

Acceptance is not always a fun thing to experience. If there is any part of this process where you will experience the paradox of the

Christian process, it is in this stage. Paul said it best in his second letter to believers in Corinth. He is talking about a "thorn in the flesh" that he asked the Lord to remove from him. Jesus responded by saying, *"My grace is sufficient for you, for my power is made perfect in weakness."* Note Paul's response to this:

> *Therefore, I will boast all the more gladly about my weaknesses, so that Christ's power may rest on me. That is why, for Christ's sake, I delight in weaknesses, in insults, in hardships, in persecutions, in difficulties. For when I am weak, then I am strong. (2 Corinthians 12:9-11 NIV)*

Stage Five: Resolution

Resolution can only be experienced when there is a conflict. And you must accept that there is a conflict before anything can be resolved. And you cannot remain angry or depressed in the middle of what may be a conflict. If you do, nothing will be resolved. And finally, the shock of all that may be occurring around you – the responsibilities, the challenges, and the idea of having to get all of these "things" organized, communicated, and accomplished – is enough to make you want to crawl into a hole. Even so, don't worry, you're in good company. We've all been there; at least I know Greg and I have. And that my friend, is why we felt moved to write about this process of growth and change in pastoral ministry and Christian leadership. Because, at some point, you will hopefully begin to realize that God is profoundly and intimately with you, even in the most disastrous and challenging times.

Remember, Jesus has experienced the depths of what the fallen world can throw at a human being. He knows what you're going through, and he knows how it feels. Sometimes that is the only thing that keeps us going. And at the risk of sounding like someone you want to get angry with, you don't know, and you don't know that you don't know until you're in the middle of it. And when you are in the middle of it, your response to "it" will be more important than what you may be going through. Remember God is with you…always, and to the ends of the earth.

Reflection Questions

- Do you believe you are right where you are supposed to be? If not, where do you believe God wants you to be except where you are? What is the alternative?

- What is your gut response to Mark's two questions? How comfortable are you knowing that you don't know what you don't know, and that your response to a crisis is critical? What would it look like to grow more comfortable with this knowledge?
- How does it make you feel to know you are not in charge, but Jesus is? What is your emotive response? What is your spiritual response?
- When is a time when you or someone you are leading was in one of these five stages? How might these stages be showing up in your life right now?

Chapter 4 – Greg

What if God's Grace is Sufficient?

*My grace is sufficient for you,
for my power is made perfect in weakness.
2 Corinthians 12:9 NIV*

Is there ever too big of a mess that we humans can make that our gracious Redeemer cannot clean up?

I DON'T KNOW ABOUT YOU, but I can make some rather large messes. Let me confess that after the senseless murder of George Floyd, I was not fully prepared to know how and when to respond. It was a crucial time for me as an individual, but as President of GCI, I knew I needed to speak on behalf of the denomination.

It was an unspoken policy that we (GCI leadership) didn't think it wise to be the first out of the gate with a response to highly emotive news events. And this event was beyond emotive. The slogan "I can't breathe" was coined as a rallying cry for what became the "Black Lives Matter" group (movement). Mark talks about our basic human responses to crisis situations – fight, flight or freeze. In this crucial moment I froze, not knowing exactly what to do.

Adding to the crisis, I received an anonymous letter that was representative of a portion of our African American Church Elders (how big of a portion I may never know). This letter decried the recent atrocities inflicted on black people, and then it surveyed historical events of our church dating back to the early 1970's, claiming that there had not been any progress in race relations and that systemic racism must be addressed. In my gut, I knew that the letter contained truths that needed attention. However, in my humanity I became defensive, and the frozen state melted into a fighting spirit. Had I not been fair in placing people into leadership roles who were called and qualified, without prejudice to gender or ethnicity? Did anybody notice that under my oversight our makeup of international Superintendents were now all indigenous leaders? Had anybody noticed the balanced composition of our denominational Board of Directors? No progress, what do you mean?

I can't claim to have close friendships with all our African American Church Elders, but I do have a large number that I have proudly served alongside and shared many life experiences with. I phoned several of these close friends, and as much as I heard their response to the letter, I didn't really hear their response. These friends brought comfort and support to me as a white man, not knowing what to think or do as I came face to face with what I didn't know I don't know. Some may call that white fragility, but my reality is that my need for a greater depth of understanding was exposed to me in this letter and those conversations. Considering the injustices and the magnitude of the moment, I should have been listening to their personal angst and pain. I should have noticed they were in their own stages of grief and attempted to process with them. Then I wouldn't have been so focused on trying to uphold my track record. Albeit these friends were bearers of God's sufficient grace to me. I will always be grateful.

It wasn't difficult for me to write to the broad GCI church family in my bi-monthly Update letter stating that "Black Lives Matter" because they do, always have and always will. The sad part is that my timing was ten days late. I see that now in hindsight. Please forgive me brothers and sisters. Through his empowering grace I hope to do better.

How has God's long arm of grace worked in and through me as we continue to address race relations and work for a better future in GCI? I have a greater awareness of what I didn't know (Mark will appreciate this "You don't know what you don't know" admission). The reading of a wide range of books regarding the major gaps in US history (I was an eighth grade US History teacher for two years of my life), and the impacts of racism was eye-opening and heart-rending. Then more poignantly, there have been field trips. A visit to the Greenwood District in Tulsa, OK where a thriving, affluent African American business community existed prior to a devasting massacre that happened in May/June 1921, when Greenwood was burned to non-existence by a mob of racist white people who were ignited by a minor incident of a young black man being accused of accosting a white female elevator operator. According to Britannica online, *"When the massacre ended on June 1, the official death toll was recorded at 10 whites and 26 African Americans, though many experts now believe at least 300 people were killed"* (an untold count of African American bodies were buried in mass graves that "somehow" became covered by highway structures). Beyond the carnage of the dead, fourteen hundred homes and businesses were burned, and nearly ten thousand people were left homeless. The amazing success of these black businessmen and women was not only destroyed, it was as if it never happened. What a huge setback for the black people of Oklahoma! And why is this part of American history left out? As we've come to find out, these were inconvenient stories which white historians omitted.

While touring the Greenwood Rising museum that commemorates the Black Wallstreet, I was alerted to another significant slice of early 20th century America. Between late winter and early autumn of 1919, there was a nationwide series of white-on-black organized attacks that took place in over three dozen US cities. This onslaught of attacks and intimidation was collectively called "Red Summer." Again, not documented in standard history textbooks.

I rejoice that there are scholars and researchers who are helping to fill in the historical gaps that paint the bigger picture of plight and struggle that our black sisters and brothers have endured. So many of these stories contain pain, death, and loss, and yet there is also struggle, victory, and deliverance. These are rich stories that make up the fabric of who we are. If you want an overview to more American stories, I commend to you a documentary created by Jeffrey Robinson, former ACLU Deputy Legal Director, entitled *Who We Are: A Chronicle of Racism in America*.

For more recent events like George Floyd and Ahmaud Arbrey, I have experienced a level of deep personal repentance. I am learning to not respond to these events like a police detective: Who did what? Why? What is the media reporting and not reporting?

When a life is lost, can I not first and foremost pause and grieve that loss? Can I consider that the family, friends, and community are impacted? Can I listen more deeply to the pain of others? Can I linger in lament instead of quickly moving through? Can my heart be broken like Jesus when he stood and cried over Jerusalem grieving their pain and loss of relationship to God due to rebellion and resistance? By

God's grace, "yes" I can to all the above. This is the incredible sufficiency and power of his grace showing up in my life to further shape and form me into the image of Jesus. Is his grace enough?

Sufficient

Sufficient is a funny word. The general meaning is "adequate" or "enough." I take this to mean "just enough," no more and no less.

Let's examine the Bible passage where the Apostle Paul states his response from God: "My grace is sufficient for you."

> *Therefore, in order to keep me from becoming conceited, I was given a thorn in my flesh, a messenger of Satan, to torment me. Three times I pleaded with the Lord to take it away from me. But he said to me, "My grace is sufficient for you, for my power is made perfect in weakness." Therefore I will boast all the more gladly about my weaknesses, so that Christ's power may rest on me. That is why, for Christ's sake, I delight in weaknesses, in insults, in hardships, in persecutions, in difficulties. For when I am weak, then I am strong. (2 Corinthians 12:7b-10 NIV)*

The most prolific Christian missionary, church-planter, and writer of the New Testament boasted in his infirmity, knowing that he couldn't take a step or breathe his next breath without God's assistance. In other Bible passages we see that Paul could clearly list his pedigree and speak of all the amazing works that Christ had done in him, and yet it is through his limitations, inadequacies, and myriad of hardships that the power of Jesus is manifest. Paul is the champion of the "not I, but Christ" posture. He walks in the footsteps of Jesus by bringing victory in mysterious ways that the world would identify as failure and defeat.

Not I, but Christ

Paul didn't start this way of course.

Have you ever considered Paul's history? He didn't start by personally pursuing a relationship with Jesus; he isn't what we would call a "seeker." In fact, Paul was a persecutor of the early church and was having Christians jailed and even killed. This was the business trip he was engaged in when Jesus abruptly revealed himself to Paul on the road to Damascus. He was still Saul when Jesus interrupted his trip and temporarily blinded him. Jesus asked the penetrating question, "Saul, how long will you persecute me?" Talk about a wake-up call!

It was Jesus who found Saul and transformed him into Paul who became the prolific Apostle. Let me suggest it is always Jesus who finds us. It his goodness and kindness that leads us to repentance, not human-engineered goodness (Romans 2:4). This is why Paul developed a posture of always – and I do mean always – referencing his complete reliance on Jesus. To believers in Galatia, he said:

> *I am crucified with Christ: nevertheless I live; yet <u>not I, but Christ</u> liveth in me: and the life which I now live in the flesh I live by the faith of the Son of God, who loved me, and gave himself for me. (Galatians 2:20 KJV)*

This is a case where the King James Version really got it right. The life found in Christ is also sustained by the faith of Jesus in the believer. It is not a self-sustaining life, rather a Jesus-dependent life. His faith, his hope, his love imparted to us, and moving us closer to being more like him.

It is important to note that Paul never forgot where he came from and what his former life was like. Note what he said to his young protégé, Timothy:

> *The grace of our Lord was poured out on me abundantly, along with the faith and love that are in Christ Jesus. Here is a trustworthy saying that deserves full acceptance: Christ Jesus came into the world to save sinners—of whom I am the worst. (1 Timothy 1:14-15 NIV)*

Paul saw himself as the chief of all sinners, and the grateful recipient of God's grace. In this personal letter he is assuring Timothy that the focused purpose of Jesus is to save sinners (all of us), and that Jesus' grace is abundant. And, if Paul himself could be saved, everybody else is salvageable too.

The more you read of Paul's letters, the more you see just how Christ-centric he is. Consider this short list of scriptures that speak to being "in Christ," and being the recipient of his grace.

> *Therefore, there is now no condemnation for those who are in Christ Jesus. (Romans 8:1 NIV)*

Therefore, if anyone is in Christ, the new creation has come: The old has gone, the new is here! (2 Corinthians 5:17 NIV)

For as in Adam all die, so in Christ all will be made alive. (1 Corinthians 15:22 NIV)

There is neither Jew nor Greek, there is neither slave nor free, there is no male and female, for you are all one in Christ Jesus. (Galatians 3:28, ESV)

And be found in him, not having a righteousness of my own that comes from the law, but that which is through faith in Christ—the righteousness that comes from God on the basis of faith. (Philippians 3:9 NIV)

His sufficient grace enables us to "be in Christ." This may seem ethereal to you, but the Bible speaks to this concept in several descriptive ways. Jesus tells Nicodemus you must be born again (John 3:3 and 5). Paul speaks to becoming a new creation (2 Corinthians 5:17). Then in his letter to the Ephesians he talks about being redeemed and adopted as sons and daughters.

When Christ saves us by the Spirit, he places us within his own sphere and joins us to him. We belong to him – as the praise song says, "I am yours, and you are mine." There is a closeness and a union that is not fragile nor dependent on our daily emotions or good works. We are united with him because of him. We are "in Christ." Hallelujah!

Delighting in Weakness

For Paul to delight in the weaknesses, insults, difficulties, and so on, you may be thinking that he was masochistic. The reality is that through his life littered with trials and persecutions, he had come to see time and time again that God's victorious grace shows up regardless of the foreboding circumstances. It wasn't the circumstances that marked Paul, rather it was the certainty of Jesus with him and in him. Jesus was and is bigger than any circumstance. Paul lived this truth, and so can we.

It was Paul's earnest desire for a mysterious thorn in his side to be removed. Scripture does not make it clear what the thorn was. Some Bible scholars speculate it was his failing eyesight causing him pain and difficulty. Others postulate he had Jewish hecklers who relentlessly followed him from city to city, causing all manner of grief. Whether it was an internal malady, or an external infliction, God's grace was still intact and sufficient to see him through. Jesus doesn't always swoop in and change our circumstance, yet he is always true to working in us and drawing us closer to himself. His grace may not remove our infirmity, but it will always cover it.

Grace is powerful and bigger than we can imagine. It is by grace that we are saved, not by anything we can do of ourselves (Ephesians 2:8-9). It is by grace that we are gifted and equipped to join Jesus in his ministry (2 Corinthians 9:8). It is grace that teaches us to say no to ungodliness and empowers us to live upright lives (Titus 2:12). To say that grace is sufficient is an understatement. Grace is more than sufficient – grace is the presence and power of Jesus to endure the storms and challenges we face, and the ability to trust and worship Jesus in the middle of every storm. Slave trader-turned-abolitionist, John Newton got it right in his song, "Amazing Grace."

Amazing Grace, how sweet the sound
That saved a wretch like me

I once was lost, but now am found
Was blind but now I see.

Allow those lyrics to run through your mind and impact your soul.

The opening to 2 Corinthians 12 is masterfully done. Paul wants his readers to know how deep and extensive his relationship has been with Jesus, even to the exposure of the glories of heaven. And yet he speaks in a veiled manner, by saying "there was a man," not fully identifying himself to be the man. Paul had to purposefully die to himself. Do we sometimes make the error of getting self in front of Jesus? For example, do we ever fixate on the spiritual gift(s) we have, then adore the gift over and above the one who is the giver of all good gifts? Our daily journey is not one that says – "Look at me. Look at me," rather it is a submissive, dependent life with our eyes fixed on Jesus telling others – "Look to Jesus, look to Jesus!" The "Not I, but Jesus" posture of Paul will serve you and me very well as we face our limitations, trials, and difficulties.

Isn't it life-changing to know that despite our frailties, shortcomings, and the messes we make, that God in his love, mercy and good pleasure reaches out to us with his all-encompassing grace? Grace does for us what we could never do for ourselves. His grace is abundantly sufficient!

Thank you, Paul, for always pointing to Jesus. We join you in the "Not I, but Christ" journey.

Reflection Questions

- In what ways has the chapter expanded your view of grace?
- What is a personal thorn in your life? How are you meeting Jesus, and Jesus meeting you in this situation?
- How can you and I go about more consistently living the posture of "Not I, but Christ" in our daily lives?

Chapter 5 – Greg

What if Longing and Yearning is God's Design for Us?

All of these died in faith without having received the promises, but from a distance they saw and greeted them. They confessed that they were strangers and foreigners on the earth, for people who speak in this way make it clear that they are seeking a homeland. If they had been thinking of the land that they had left behind, they would have had opportunity to return. But as it is, they desire a better country, that is, a heavenly one. Therefore God is not ashamed to be called their God; indeed, he has prepared a city for them.
Hebrews 11:13-16 NRSV

THIS LONG LIST OF BIBLE HEROES had a common theme. They were looking forward, waiting for, and eagerly expecting a God-built homeland. They confessed that they were strangers, knowing their citizenship was not in this world. These champions of faith expressed an ardent yearning and deep longing through want and grief, persecution and torture with their distant hope in the forefront of their thinking.

If this was their lot in this life, then why not ours as well? Are we longing and yearning for the fulfillment when all citizenship is under the one banner of Jesus Christ? Do we set our minds on and yearn for what the Lord is preparing for us beyond the noise and distractions of this present world?

A major challenge for "Kingdom Citizens" arises when our passions become entangled with deep associations with our country and our particular people group. According to research from Florian Bieber, "Over the past years, rising nationalism[1] is seen everywhere and in everything. From the election of Donald Trump to Brexit, the nationalist policies of the Japanese Prime Minister Shinzō Abe, his Indian counterpart Narendra Modi, and the Turkish president Recep Tayyip Erdoğan, the success of far-right parties in Italian, German and Austrian elections in 2017 and 2018, nationalism appears to be on the rise globally."[2]

The real danger to nationalistic politics is its exclusionary and virulent sides. In the Christian realm, mixing nationalism with Christianity creates a complex stew that can easily distort what being Christian means. This was quite a struggle for American Christians through the Trump presidency, leading to the controversial storming of the U.S. Capitol building.

The Capitol Building incident provided a rare occasion when a television star gave sound advice that points us back to the foundation of our forefathers and foremothers of Hebrews 11. After the riot at the U.S. Capitol, the news was dominated by alarming stories on the left and right ahead of the Jan. 20 presidential inauguration. On that Friday, actress Patricia Heaton (*Everybody Loves Raymond*, and *The Middle*), took to Twitter to lament that common sense is hard to find right now. *"If you're a common sense person, you probably don't feel you have a home in this world right now,"* she wrote. *"If you're a Christian, you know you were never meant to."* (Fox News Flash, January 9, 2021).

"Our home is not found in this world" was a grounding word of advice I needed to hear during that stressful time. Rather than "Make America Great Again," what if we were to join the chorus of the faithful in Hebrews 11 and declare "God's Kingdom is Already Great"? What if we lived as responsible citizens in our native land, and held the same mindset as the cloud of witnesses who have gone before? Are our

---

[1] The main problem with nationalism is it is not Kingdom focused. The difference between isolationist/nationalism and globalism is important to understand because neither are Kingdom focused. The radicalization of extreme nationalism, superiority and arrogance reflects Babylonian (world ruling) thinking, but extreme globalism has a Tower of Babel mindset that must also be acknowledged. The only answer is Kingdom Citizenry but too many Christians have become divided by right (nationalistic) and left (globalistic) heresies and have taken their eyes off Jesus and his Kingdom.

[2] Is Nationalism on the Rise? Assessing Global Trends, Florian Bieber, Pages 519-540 (Published online: 24 Oct 2018).

minds tuned to the kingdom whose maker and builder is the Triune God of the Bible? Our allegiance to the right cause matters.

The theme of longing and yearning in the Hebrews 11 account spilled over to all the persons listed in the "Believer's Hall of Fame." I would add that it spills over to all generations of Christ followers.

I recently took the LivStyle personality assessment, and my Biblical profile equates me to Nehemiah, the visionary whose purpose was to rebuild the walls of Jerusalem after the Israelite exile to Babylon. As I researched this Old Testament story, I came upon Dr. Tim Mackie's explanations in his work "The Bible Project." This clever graphic-based presentation shows how the work of Nehemiah was parallel to the works of Zerubbabel and Ezra. Zerubbabel's work was the rebuilding of the temple, which fell short because it didn't have the glory of the original temple. Ezra attempted to restore spiritual and social renewal, which bogged down over the matter of mixed marriages between Israelites and non-Israelites. Then Nehemiah, sponsored by Persian King Artaxerxes, organized the Israelites to rebuild the walls and gates around Jerusalem. He worked with individual families to encourage each family to build the section of wall in their "backyard." The wall was getting built, but again the work bogged down because the spiritual condition of the people did not change.

These three Old Testament leaders entered their work with high hopes and promise, and yet in each case the work was done with measured success and ended in disappointment. The underlying theme throughout the Old Testament is the need for a Messiah. They needed a deliverer who could do more than change the sociopolitical ills; they needed a deliverer who could transform the hearts of humans and deliver them from the clutches of sin.

Fortunately for us, we live on "the right side of the cross." Our Messiah has come and conquered sin and death and brought about the reality that we can be "new creations" in him. And because we await his second coming, we live in a state called "the already, but not yet."

"Already, but not yet" describes the tension between the redemption already experienced in this life because of Jesus, and the glorification yet to come at the consummation. As born-again Christians, we enjoy the "already-ness" of the Atonement—forgiveness of sins, adoption as children, the indwelling of the Holy Spirit, and inclusion in the Book of Life. And yet, the full realization of all we are in Christ is in the future. For example, Ephesians 2:6 tells us that we are raised with Jesus and seated in the heavenly realm with him. This is true because of who Jesus is and how he has included us, yet, just like you, I am physically present in my brick-and-mortar house on planet earth. In like manner, the church is a fellowship of people who are new creatures in Christ (saints), and still human and subject to temptation and moral failure (sinners). The Apostle Paul says it best to believers in Rome:

> *I consider that the sufferings of this present time are not worth comparing with the glory about to be revealed to us. For the creation waits with eager longing for the revealing of the children of God, for the creation was subjected to futility, not of its own will, but by the will of the one who subjected it, in hope that the creation itself will be set free from its enslavement to decay and will obtain the freedom of the glory of the children of God. We know that the whole creation has been groaning together as it suffers together the pains of labor, and not only the creation, but we ourselves, who have the first fruits of the Spirit, groan inwardly while we wait for adoption, the redemption of our bodies. For in hope we were saved. Now hope that is seen is not hope, for who hopes for what one already sees? But if we hope for what we do not see, we wait for it with patience. (Romans 8:18-25 NRSVUE).*

Yearning and longing amidst discomfort and travail is by God's design. This is not for futility or waste, rather for the higher good that God is working out – the complete redemption of humanity and all of creation.

Author Dr. Gerald G. May in his book, *Addiction and Grace* says this:

> "In our society, we have come to believe that discomfort always means something is wrong. We are conditioned to believe that feelings of distress, pain, deprivation, yearning, and longing mean something is wrong with the way we are living our lives. Conversely, we are convinced that a rightly lived life must give us serenity, completion, and fulfillment. Comfort means "right" and distress means "wrong." The influence of such convictions is stifling to the human spirit. Individually and collectively, we must somehow recover the truth. The truth is, we were never meant to be completely satisfied."

As paradoxical as it may seem, the Lord, in his infinite wisdom, knows that hoping, waiting, and longing, in spite of our circumstances, is part of our development to bring us to glory. The earlier a young believer can grasp hold of this truth, the more likely he or she will solidify their allegiance to Jesus and his eternal kingdom. More likely they will find kinship with the good people of Hebrews 11.

Conclusion

This chapter may feel ironic. "Hey Greg and Mark, why do you promise me a building up of hope, and then bring me to this point of promising a life with the need for sustained hope clothed in longing and yearning?" We do live in a world filled with hurt, and we have a yearning for healing and hope. Mark will address this more in the next chapter as he discusses the first step of the healing process.

Hopefully, you are growing more comfortable with being uncomfortable. I hope you are encouraged with the reality that being Christian pilgrims on this earth is our shared calling; we are all in this uncomfortableness together. Our pilgrimage is wrapped in the communion with Jesus through the Spirit and alongside our brothers and sisters of the church. The deep longing in our hearts to be in the fullness of God's eternal kingdom burns brightly no matter our present circumstance. Growing comfortable in the discomfort of longing and yearning is normative for the believer whose eyes are fixed on Jesus. Collectively, we await our glorification and the final transformation of our sinful natures. In that "last day" we will be face-to-face with our King and friend, Jesus the Christ and "the not yet," will become "now…and forever."

Jesus really is the head of his church, and he really is the King of the eternal Kingdom!

Reflection Questions

- In what ways has your Christian worldview been challenged by cultural biases or societal influences?
- Read through Hebrews chapter 11. How do you relate to any of these characters and their circumstances?
- Have you experienced a long-term desire that remains unfulfilled? What has the hoping and waiting process been like for you?
- How do you experience Jesus in the "already?" What are you longing for in the "not yet?"

What if Jesus...

Chapter 6 – Mark

What if Jesus Knows the Reality of Life...

...and our tendency to live in denial?

I have been crucified with Christ and I no longer live, but Christ lives in me. The life I now live in the body, I live by faith in the Son of God, who loved me and gave himself for me.
Galatians 2:20 NIV

IN FEBRUARY OF 2020, I was with Greg and Randy Bloom, our current GCI Board Chair, at a Regional Directors cabin retreat in Ohio. COVID-19 was quickly becoming a reality. On the way to the airport to return home, I had Jeff Broadnax, one of our Regional Directors, stop at a grocery store so I could purchase disinfecting wipes and hand sanitizer. Our reality was changing fast, and there was nothing that any of us could do to stop it.

When I arrived at the airport in Cincinnati, I felt as if I was in the middle of a post-Apocalyptic movie. The airport was basically empty except for a few hundred, maybe up to a thousand, brave souls who were trying to get home. As I walked to my gate, I saw less than ten people in the concourse. Again, I had never experienced anything like this before. I called Debra and tried to explain to her what I was experiencing, but all I could really do was tell her what I was seeing. In retrospect that experience was beyond words.

When I arrived home in Houston, people in the airport were moving fast and not talking to one another. There was a look of intense unsureness on everyone's faces. I quickly found my bags, was picked up by Deb, and we headed for our home just fifteen minutes away.

Within one week of arriving home, the entire Houston metro area, along with most of the country was put on lock-down. Debra and I looked at each other...and at first, we thought... "let's do this, we can adjust." And then reality started to settle in.

Due to my counseling licenses and the nature of Deb's job (she is a director for a large medical group; she's in charge of hiring their physicians), reality set in very fast. My counseling practice had to completely change to telehealth. Deb's office building was shut down. Despite these drastic changes, we were expected to keep on going at the same pace. Deb and I are very active. We received a notification via email that our regular health club was now closed until further notice. All the restaurants that we frequented every Friday for our traditional "date night" also closed. In fact, everything seemed to be closing except grocery stores, Walmart, and liquor stores. I now had to wait in line to enter our local grocery store. We had to wear masks, and we had to stand six feet apart on stickers that were now on the sidewalks. The shelves inside the store were not as full as before, and people were now going into "hoarding" mode. And this was just the beginning.

Deb began to get calls from her employees. Their kids were now at home; schools were closed and attempting to adjust to online teaching. These parents/employees suddenly had to make astronomical adjustments no one saw coming. And as if that wasn't bad enough, I started getting calls to see if I had any openings for new patients in my counseling practice. And these weren't just mild cases of anxiety or situational depression. People's lives were being torn apart. Marriages were breaking up; young people were now "crashing" – emotionally, educationally, and relationally. Parents had no idea how to cope with what was turning out to be a total disruption of schedules, structure, and life in general. It seemed nothing was left untouched. It will be beyond interesting to read future studies that demonstrate the impact this period of history had on our global community.

And then there was our church. The building where we were meeting closed immediately, no questions asked. Fortunately, we were already doing "Facebook live," so we scrambled to get the word out that we were now only going to have sermons online.

Our lives were not supposed to be affected this way! As I would sit and ponder this new frame of "reality" that was changing daily, the words my dad had said to me in the past chimed inside my head...

"Mark, that's what you get for thinking." I used to get so mad when dad would say that phrase, but this experience, along with many others, re-enforced something that I must pray about every morning to accept. Simply stated, I am not in charge. In fact, none of us are in charge of much of anything. This was Paul's point to the believers in Galatia. As much as he may have wanted to be in charge (and I'm not saying he did), Paul knew it was Jesus who was in control and thank God he is. Paul learned to trust that all good was in and through Christ, who we want/need to be in charge. And if I have learned anything more deeply because of COVID, it is the reality that I am not in control, and joining Paul, I say, thank God for that. As we say in recovery, I am powerless. And when life hits us with this reality, it is shocking; our first tendency may be to deny that it is actually happening.

As I write, it's now February 28, 2022. The news is now showing nothing but the Russian invasion of the Ukraine, as if COVID wasn't enough. And as I look on my phone to see what the stock market is doing…well, who knows. So, here's the question. Why do we as humans experience shock and denial?

According to most physicians and mental health workers, we were created with the ability to survive intense, emotional experiences by almost regressing to three base behaviors. As Greg mentioned in the previous chapter, they are fight, flight, or freeze. Again, these are very base (limbic) responses that find their origins in a part of our brain called the "limbic system." This is the part of our brain that will "take over" during experiences like being in a car crash, being attacked, being in war, sudden news of the death of a loved one, or being told that one has a terminal disease. In my opinion, most everyone has had one of these experiences. And some have experienced them more intensely than others. And if one has not experienced them intensely, being a pastor or a ministerial leader will open the door for a person to have that experience, either in a literal fashion, or vicariously.

But what most people don't realize is that it is possible to be in what would be considered a "milder" state of fight, flight, or freeze. And when that happens, things can really get interesting. This milder state may possibly manifest itself in various "presentations" that we call anxiety, depression, and a myriad of other "states" that we as humans have named. Now, I'm not saying this is the reason for all the individuals who present this way. Even so, this book is focusing on those that want to serve in Christian leadership. And when Pastor B realizes that the "job" may be much more challenging than he originally considered (back to the first of the two phrases), it can literally be a shock. So, he may start trying to put in more time, get to know his leaders better. Sometimes this works, and sometimes it doesn't. And as he does this, he may start expecting those closest to him (his family) to "give" so that he can do God's work. If that is the case, then he may be in a state of denial of what is really going on and how he is truly feeling.

That, my friends, is what has brought most full-time pastors into my clinical office for help. They feel that something is wrong, and they just can't put their finger on it. The fact is, they start trying to live for everyone else, and they expect their families to understand how much they "love" these people, and how much it is their "calling" to make sure everyone is "OK."

Something Needs to Change:

In my opinion, there are basically four phases people go through as they experience change. (I mentioned these in the introduction, but it bears repeating for this chapter.) The first is *knowledge*. The second is *acceptance*, i.e., are they teachable so that they can learn that what they think they know isn't working. If they accept this new knowledge, it will "reframe" the *experience*, the third phase. In fact, everything they have and are currently experiencing may be looked at differently. The final stage of change is *trust*; new knowledge that is accepted changes your experiences and you may have to consider who you can now trust, including yourself.

It is important to understand that grieving is normal during certain stages of change and development in life. Many people have told me it feels like they are "dying on the inside." And that, my friends, is the "shock" stage of change – as you begin to grieve the reality that you have no idea what to do in the context of what you are experiencing. And this happens often in leadership. So, you can either fight, run, simply shut down – or you can realize that you are in shock because things are not going the way you thought they were going to go. Another way of putting this is you are not getting what you want the way you want.

The Gospels relay a story where one of the members of the Sanhedrin, a Pharisee named Nicodemus, sneaks out in the middle of the night to meet with Jesus in person. The crux of the conversation is that Nicodemus wants to know what Jesus is really teaching. Jesus comes up with the phrase, "You must be born again." Nicodemus interprets this phrase literally, and in a humorous exchange challenges Jesus on the physical and anatomical impossibility of this even happening. But, as we now know, Jesus was speaking metaphorically. As Christians, we must be "born again."

Let's have some fun. Let's think this through. If I, as I now am, must be "born again," doesn't that mean that my current self must die? If there is one thing we all know for sure, it is that we are all going to physically die. But is that what Jesus is talking about? I don't think so. If it is a metaphor, then how does a living person experience being "born again"? Could it be that everything that this living person thinks they need in order to live must actually die?

In other words, everything we think to be normal, everything we think we know, might have to be challenged. And as this happens, it may not always be easy to accept. And, if it is not easy to accept, then we must admit we may be in denial regarding some aspects of our lives.

If someone or something comes along and makes our lives feel like we are being tested, what may be happening is that God is giving us the opportunity to learn something new. But if we are not teachable, we may not be able to accept that what we think is a trial may be a time to learn. If this doesn't cross our minds, and we are trying to "fix" something or make the trial go away, then denial may be our reality at that time. Either way, we will probably grieve. One reason is because we're not getting what we want; the other reason is because change is never easy… at some point it feels like you're dying on the inside. You know when I think about it, I've never talked to a woman who told me that her literal birthing pains were wonderful. In fact, women have told me about the pain of birthing their first child…it was literally "shocking" pain.

What would be wise to consider if you are in Christian Leadership is that this scenario will be your new normal. Here are some "must learn" lessons for Christian leaders:

- Accepting that you are not in charge.
- Accepting that this is not your ministry, it belongs to Jesus.
- Accepting that you will be challenged to the core on dynamics in life that you didn't even know could be challenging (those phrases again).

- Accepting that no matter how distraught, discouraged and rejected you may feel, you are not what you are experiencing or feeling…in God's eyes at least.
- Accepting these truths is overwhelmingly challenging.

It is shocking to experience, and it is easy to resort to denying these principles as true. Most of us have denied them as true as we go through this process. And then, something happens. It's like you're at a crossroads. And it doesn't mean it's going to make us feel better. It means you have come to the point of acceptance. And that brings us to the next reality of grieving during change.

Reflection Questions

- How did the COVID pandemic bring shock to your world?
- Consider something you are currently going through and ask what phase are you in: knowledge, acceptance, experience, or trust?
- In what area of your life do you feel like you are sinking?
- How does your approach to ministry and leadership change knowing you are not in charge?

Chapter 7 - Greg

What if Jesus Really Understands the Human State (Us)...

...and his primary mission all along has been to set the captives (us) free?

When he came to Nazareth, where he had been brought up, he went to the synagogue on the sabbath day, as was his custom. He stood up to read, and the scroll of the prophet Isaiah was given to him. He unrolled the scroll and found the place where it was written: "The Spirit of the Lord is upon me, because he has anointed me to bring good news to the poor. He has sent me to proclaim release to the captives and recovery of sight to the blind, to let the oppressed go free, to proclaim the year of the Lord's favor." And he rolled up the scroll, gave it back to the attendant, and sat down. The eyes of all in the synagogue were fixed on him. Then he began to say to them, "Today this scripture has been fulfilled in your hearing."
Luke 4:16-20 NRSV

THIS IS JESUS' "DROP THE MIC" MOMENT. The passage he reads from Isaiah completely articulates his mission. The *Commentary Critical and Explanatory on the Whole Bible* says this:

"He (Jesus) selects a passage announcing the sublime object of His whole mission, its divine character, and His special endowments for it; expressed in the first person, and so singularly adapted to the first opening of the mouth in His prophetic capacity, that it seems as if made expressly for this occasion."[3]

Jesus spoke words of deliverance to a broken society. He covers the gamut of human suffering from poverty, captivity, and bodily afflictions, to being broken-hearted and crushed. Through the power of the Spirit, Jesus is the messenger of good news, the proclaimer of release, the healer of physical afflictions, and the true liberator for the oppressed. He was and is the glorious Messiah and Healer that Israel was expecting.

Why then, do we sometimes feel broken and so in need of healing? Perhaps you see yourself in need of good news. Is there anything holding you captive? Do you need healing in your body? Do you need healing in your spirit? Are you experiencing oppression of any kind? Ultimately, do you need a Messiah who can heal you?

Over the past several years, our GCI leaders have been in the healthy routine of having cabin retreats. These four-day gatherings allow space for rich discussions, meaningful planning, and relational bonding in an environment that cannot be duplicated in an office board room or a hotel conference room. Sharing living space, preparing meals together, and just sitting around surrounded by the quiet and beauty of nature, is the perfect combination to collaborate, gain clarity, and to move forward together.

You are probably thinking, "Why is he talking about cabin retreats? I thought we were on the theme of living in brokenness and needing a deliverer?" Allow me to tie these thoughts together. One of the most moving and liberating activities of the cabin retreat is a prayer exercise called "The Chair." We place a chair in the middle of the room and one by one each participant moves into the chair as he or she is ready and willing. The person in the chair prays a prayer for himself and then the colleagues pray additional prayers over the person in the chair. This sounds normative for a group of Christian leaders. What's the big deal?

The big deal is that when we first began this process, each person prefaced their journey to the chair by saying something like, "Oh I don't have that much going on. Not a lot to pray about." Then one by one each participant began bearing their soul in front of God and their

---

[3] Jamieson, R., Fausset, A. R., & Brown, D. (1997). *Commentary Critical and Explanatory on the Whole Bible* (Vol. 2, p. 103). Oak Harbor, WA: Logos Research Systems, Inc.

friends. The prayers were so transparent and the depth of sharing more than we had ever experienced with one another. Through the unction of the Spirit, we were acknowledging deep levels of brokenness, and then collectively we were meeting the liberator Jesus in ways none of us had experienced before.

I recall the time when I was just stepping into my role as church president. As I began praying for myself, I began thinking about how the demands of the job could become a major obstacle from my ability to spend time with my children and my infant grandchildren. I didn't want to be that leader who was known and loved by the church folk, while a stranger to his own family. As I prayed for God's wisdom and the guidance of the Spirit, it totally caught me off guard how gut-wrenched I was about this overwhelming angst related to my role as husband, father, and grandfather. I found myself sobbing to the point that the words would no longer come out. The brothers around me picked up the prayers at this point and continued to lift me to the mercy seat of heaven. We repeated a similar process for each leader.

That day we spent nearly the entire afternoon in prayer. We went through at least one box of tissue, and we were all physically exhausted. Physically spent, yet spiritually rejuvenated. This was a day of captives experiencing release. It was a day when a group of Christian men who thought that "all was well" discovered that really meeting Jesus was about surrendering the inside stuff. That stuff we very much like to keep buried. Being honest and open about one's brokenness and neediness is the pathway to freedom.

Freedom From

It is about what we are free from AND what we are free for. These are two sides of the same coin.

In Luke 4, we hear Jesus proclaiming:
Freedom from dominance and abuse.
Freedom from being impoverished.
Freedom from physical debilitating maladies.

These are the forces and conditions that make life especially difficult. These are the forces that no human is immune from. Jesus knows that we humans need healing and release, and he knows and wants us to know that he is the one, true source for that healing and release.

The physical conditions listed above also have spiritual implications – spiritual captivity, spiritual bankruptcy, and spiritual blindness. The culture of liberation that Jesus was really getting at as he lived out his life ministering to Jews and Gentiles throughout Israel, was a freeing from sin, death, guilt, and shame.

As much as the oppression of the Roman rulership with its taxes and bullying was deeply felt by the people of Christ's day, their ultimate deliverance was not from Rome. The ultimate deliverance was from sin and its consequence of death, and the renewing of the mind that lifts the oppression of guilt and shame that sin brings. When a person has experienced spiritual renewal in Jesus, facing the hardships of the human experience becomes a whole new ballgame.

Freedom For

Freedom in Jesus is the freedom to be indwelt by the Holy Spirit, become an adopted child of God, and have our natures being renewed. In Jesus, we are free to become the best versions of ourselves. This is freedom for a transformed, empowered life.

Freedom in Jesus is an invitation to join him as witnesses in this world to the Good News about Jesus Christ, who alone is Lord and Savior, and is alone to be worshipped. We are free to join him and participate in much of what he is doing.

We are free to grow in relationship with Jesus and with one another. After all, the eternal kingdom of God is about loving, harmonious relationships in a world free of sin, sorrow, and pain.

We are free to see how he is at work in people around us. Seeing the light of Jesus shining in and through others is one of life's greatest joys.

We are free to share his love that he has liberally bestowed on us. God is love and we are free to bask in it, and lavish it onto others.

Challenges of Freedom

Christian freedom also brings unique challenges in how we responsibly exercise our freedom. In a candid conversation with Dr. Gary Deddo, he said the following.

> "What we are freed for, in the Gospel of Jesus Christ, really does prevent a secular co-option of what Jesus was proclaiming – about himself. We are not freed from living in the present evil age, we are not freed from having to hope in the end of this age and Christ's

return. We are not freed from rendering to God what alone is God's, and only rendering to Caesar what can be claimed as his. We are not freed to use any means to bring about a potential human ideal. We are not freed, as the church, to surrender the Lordship of Christ to any other lord or to hope that a kingdom of human engineering will be, become, or turn into the kingdom of God."

Being free in Jesus is also being fully dependent on Jesus. Constantly looking to him for wisdom. Talking to him about everything – the good, the bad and the messy. Rejoicing with him over our greatest victories and joys. Sharing with him our deepest hurts and fears. Relying on him for our every need – even our next breath. To truly be free is to be completely surrendered to Jesus.

Concluding Thoughts

So, what if Jesus has brought salvation to all those in need: poor, blind, and captive? This would represent restored property, restored health, and freedom from outside rule. Perhaps the people of that day would've been satisfied with this (maybe us too). However, his presence means more. It means release from bondage, and specifically bondage rooted in the activity of Satan that leads humanity into the works of anger, hate, strife, and so on.

Setting the captives free is more than opening a cell door. True freedom only comes in a surrendered life to the one who is truly King and Messiah, and whose influence fills the liberated captives with love, joy, peace, and so on. It is the freedom to be in eternal relationship to the King!

Reflection Questions

- Have you ever thought of yourself as a captive who needs liberating?
- What makes it so easy to internally bury the deep issues? (Consider the example of Greg and his surprise over the deep angst about his role as husband, father and grandfather.)
- Thinking through your life experiences, what freedom from Jesus' mission statement in Luke 4 has made the biggest impression in your relationship with him?
- How do we live as Kingdom citizens even while we live as natural citizens in our earthy home countries?

What if Jesus...

Chapter 8 – Mark (and Greg)

What if Jesus' Love Really is Enough?

Wretched man that I am! Who will rescue me from this body of death? Thanks be to God through Jesus Christ our Lord!
Romans 7:24-25 NRSVA

HAVE YOU EVER STRUGGLED in the same way Paul did? We can answer for you. We know what we want to do, and we don't do it. We do the things we don't want to do. We find ourselves in vicious cycles that can lead to struggles with self-worth and depression. We finally come to that point that Paul came to. "I can't do this. I need to be rescued. Who can rescue me before this kills me?"

The point of this book is not to tell you how to work your way out of this cycle, but to look to the One who does rescue us. Thanks be to Jesus. He is the rescuer, but how does this rescue look? We'd love it if Jesus would just take away the sinful thoughts and actions, and we'd love for him to give us a new body now, but that's not how he works. Let's look at how he does work. And the best way we can do that is share some of our experiences.

As you read in the introduction, when Greg wanted me to write this book, my head said, "No way Dude!", but my heart said "yes." As we have stressed throughout the book, Greg and I are very different. I'm one of those guys who suffers from "analysis paralysis" more times than I'd like to admit. I've forgotten my Myers Briggs letters, but I finally succumbed to taking the enneagram and scored as an off the charts "9," with a wing of "8" that is just a few percentage points behind. This is considered a unique group and the personality type is called, "The Referee." I'm considered "confident, bold, and motivating."

Regarding my "Livstyle" profile, I am primarily a "Refiner" and under pressure a "Pragmatist." A very wise woman I know told me of a t-shirt she bought for a relative that said, "Give me fifteen minutes, I have to overthink this before I decide!" That's me. Ironically, my wife Debra is like a female version of Greg, so I guess opposites truly do attract. You ought to hear the two of them talk when Greg visits; most would be running out of the room. Even so, I truly love my wife and have grown over the years to truly appreciate and love her more despite our vast differences. And that brings me to Greg.

According to the "GIANT™" statistics Greg refers to in his chapters, more than 70% of the general population are what's called nurturers or guardians. Greg, identifying himself as a pioneer, fits into less than 10% of the general population. When you read his chapters, you might say, "this guy sounds like a general rallying the troops." He comes across as an idealist with a can-do spirit. As a pioneer, he is all of that, but he's also a realist and that's why he wanted me to partner with him in writing this book. He wanted the voice of a nurturer. He wanted my voice because of the experience and training I have that he does not have. That humility speaks volumes to me and encouraged me to agree.

As I was coached by Denny Howard using my "Livstyle" profile, Denny stated something to the order of, "Mark, you're the perfect counselor; you can feel with your heart and keep your head in the moment at the same time." Yes, that is a gift the Holy Spirit gave me, and I love working with people. But, if you're a church leader – which I am – it often *feels like* you have to do much more than just stay in the moment. You have to have a vision and mission, you have to consider how to develop leaders, delegate, collaborate, be an example, and live in, with, around, by, for, and because of Jesus. Further, you are expected to stand alongside people and their families during times of trauma or trial. It's exhausting! It simply doesn't make sense. How can something that seems so loving and unbelievably good, simple and true, burn so many church leaders, wives, and families out to the point of feeling like they are total failures? It all has to do with love. But the key is knowing whose love we are talking about.

In 1 John 4, we read two amazing statements. First, in verses 8 and 16 we read, "God is love." Second, in verse 19 we read, "We love because he first loved us."

John is writing some sixty years after the death and resurrection of Jesus to the first century church who were being challenged by thoughts and ideas rooted in human philosophies. His message was simple. And that, my friends, will always be my struggle. I simply have to remind myself that the gospel is really that simple. We love him and others because he loved us first. In fact, it's so simple, I try to think my way out of it almost every hour of every day; sometimes more. We love because of who he is – love, and because he lives in us. So, we love with his love because we are loved.

What is love? Is it a feeling? If it is, that could be a problem. Not only with you, but also for Jesus. Why? Well, do you always "like" the ones that you're supposed to "love"? Do you think Jesus felt wonderful when he was on the cross? He cried out, "My God, my God, why have you forsaken me?" as a reminder to himself that he was not in control; he was in the Father's hands. I don't believe Jesus felt good as he looked down from the Mount of Olives and sobbed...lamenting the unbelief and lack of faith of this "city" that had persecuted and tortured some of the prophets, and knowing they were going to do the very same thing to him. I can't help but wonder how Jesus felt about his disciples when he came down from the transfiguration, only to be confronted by a man whose son had been taken to the disciples for healing and it didn't work. He basically said, "How long do I have to put up with these people?" Have you ever asked someone how they're doing and when they answered "blessed," you just wanted to slap them? For our sake, we better pray that love is not a feeling. If it is, it seems we all may be condemned, including Jesus. With what I read in the Gospels, Jesus didn't always "feel" good.

The Greek word for God's love is "agape." According to the Encyclopedia Britannica, *agape* is defined as the "fatherly love of God towards humans." If this is the case, let's think this through: God had to love us first with a fatherly love towards humans, and then, and only then, can we love anyone else? What? That seems the opposite of what many are taught, yet anyone who is a parent knows this to be true. We love our children long before they are able to reciprocate any kind of love. Why then are so many Christians taught that they have to first love God with all their heart, or their lives will be a mess and they'll "suffer" until they learn to do this?

This logic/faith, leads to setting a personal goal to "love God more." In the context of this book, your church might have a vision and mission to learn to "love God more," and so you teach the leaders, members, and new attendees that the vision of your church is "to learn to love God more." Great! Now, who starts first? In other words, who's in charge of the "mission and vision?" Whose perspective is going to be the foundation on which all of the congregation's members will work on loving God more? Let's take it further; if you let someone accept this role, then that individual has just been given the power to judge everyone else in the church (except himself or herself, because they're now in charge), on how others are doing with learning to love God more. Oh yes, I want to belong to that church...sign me up! I know this sounds rude and sarcastic, and, full disclosure, I did join that church and thrived.

In September of 1979, at the age of eighteen, I was baptized into what was then known as "The Worldwide Church of God." I was "learning to love God more." How? By keeping the law. You see, starting my junior year in high school, I started keeping the seventh-day Sabbath. I refused to work at any job from Friday sunset to Saturday sunset. I also stopped eating pork, shrimp, catfish, and anything else listed in Leviticus 11 and Deuteronomy 14 as "unclean." I stopped observing Christmas and Easter. I started keeping what was called the "Holy Days." I began to tithe...a lot. Ten percent to the church, along with another ten percent in a savings account to be spent in its entirety during an eight-day festival in the fall. And every third year, an extra ten percent went to "Headquarters" for additional assistance for support of widows and orphans. I was accepted as a student at the church's private college, where I became BMOC (big man on campus). I was given leadership positions, sent out as a ministerial trainee during my junior and senior year, and our founder and "Pastor General" asked for me by name in several contexts. Everyone expected me to be hired right out of college into full time ministry. But there was a problem.

You see, this is also where I met Debra. What you don't know, is that we became very involved early on, and you just didn't do that at this college. It was against the rules. What else you don't know is that Debra was told that due to her strong personality (she's like Greg...remember), she was not going to be a good "pastor's wife." As you can guess, I was not hired into the ministry.

After graduation, I got a job in sales. I lost that job in less than three years. Then I was hired as an assistant pastor...finally. We both thought that "the blessings" were finally being poured out upon us. But then, personal illnesses were discovered – six surgeries in seven years for Deb, two for me. Dual infertility...adoption of two wonderful children – they are biological brother and sister (the process was gut wrenching). Then in 1995, the "Worldwide Church of God" began to change all its basic doctrines. And of course, I went along with the changes. As a result, the local membership in our churches was decimated.

This led to Deb and I experiencing significant financial struggles. In the midst of all this, I was called out for being a masterful co-dependent and was told I was the one who needed help. What??? I was just trying to teach my family how to love God. That way our "suffering" would end – or at least lessen – and we could finally be blessed. How dare you tell me I don't care and don't love others! In recovery terms, accepting that I was the one that felt and thought that I had the power, experience, and knowledge to teach others how to "love God" was my "rock bottom."

You see, I had to accept, and be reminded daily, that no matter how much I cared for others, no matter how many hours and hours I was willing to give to our church members, I was not the one who had the power to change their hearts. Oh, I could guilt and shame them into changing their behavior out of threat of being condemned and lost, but that is not changing one's heart. To do that, the relationship has to be safe, with no conditions, and no expectations. It has to be based on *agape* and exemplified in grace.

When I meet the apostle Paul in heaven – yes, I do believe I'll be there – I want to ask him a lot of questions. In Romans 7:14-25 we find, in my opinion, one of the most paradoxical, gut wrenching, honest passages in the New Testament. Paul just "lays it out." In laymen's terms he basically says, "I don't do what I know I should, I do the things I shouldn't do, I can't stop it...I've tried, it doesn't work...it's so bad, it is a law of "sin and death inside of me." Now, at the risk of sounding like a little snot, does Paul need to "learn to love God more" so this can be "fixed" inside of him and he will be delivered from his sufferings and finally be blessed? If my studies are correct, Paul wrote this passage some twenty-two years after he was converted. Let that sink in – twenty-two years. What does this mean?

Following the twenty-fifth verse in Romans 7, Paul, after thanking God for Jesus and in spite of what he just personally admitted he knows exists in his "being," gives us the answer to this paradox in all of chapter 8. But, unless you read Romans 7:14-25, chapter 8 can come across as something you have to "do" or "learn more about." Instead, it's simply a personal testimony from a man who had to live with the fact that he had arrested, jailed, and probably killed the very people that he has now humbly accepted the responsibility to teach. What is he teaching? God's love. But Paul had to come to the most horribly terrifying reality regarding God's love. He didn't deserve it!

Do you get that? The Apostle Paul, the one God called to share the gospel with the Gentiles, came to realize he did not deserve God's love. What does that say about us? Well, there's more to the story here.

Paul miraculously accepted God's love. God's love – loving God with all your heart, mind, and soul, and loving your neighbor as yourself – is not something you learn; it is God's gift to us. It is offered with no conditions, even to the ones that least deserve it (in our eyes, not God's). God loves and will always love Paul. That's the truth Paul learned to accept. Even if it didn't make sense, he knew it to be true. I believe that's one reason Paul resorted to the word "mystery" when referring to this love we call "The Gospel."

So, what about you? As a church leader, are you beginning to realize that you cannot offer what you have not clearly accepted you may first need for yourself? Are you trying to hide behind your family and church members because you really know what's inside of you and it scares you to death? If you are in ministry to try to "make up" for the wrongs you feel you've done to yourself or others, or because you're trying to "make things right," you will crash and burn, and God will let you. Not because you're being punished, but because he loves you. It's not a failure; remember, there are no conditions when it comes to God's love. It may be that he has already given you something you will never be able to give yourself, no matter how much you serve, or how hard you try – and believe me, I tried. He is giving you total, unconditional forgiveness and more.

He looks at you and sees the resurrected Jesus. He is not holding your sins against you; they simply don't exist in his reality of you. You now have a new identity; it's more than just having your sins forgiven. You cannot love unless you take the risk to let him love you despite how you feel about yourself. Love is not a feeling, it is an action, a verb, and God did it and has always done it for you perfectly. You cannot, nor will you ever be able to love in the way that God loves you.

When you accept this, then and only then will you begin to understand what it means to love others. It seems like something we have to "do." That's the paradox that is so confusing. But we don't do it; it seems we just start to experience it. And it's usually not because we are feeling good. Can it really be that simple? YES! If you don't believe me, read openly and honestly about Jesus and Paul...they felt the same way you do right now. You are not alone.

Comments From Greg

We are now midway through the book, and I am inserting myself into Mark's chapter. Mark's revelation about his journey as a teenager into what was the Worldwide Church of God and Ambassador College was a parallel journey that he and I share almost identically (with the exception that he was from Kansas, and I was from North Carolina). Giving up shrimp and shellfish was one of the biggies for me and my family (I have been making up for that deficit since 1995).

Mark and I differentiate in the order of our five voices, but we find a parcel of common ground in the Enneagram. I am a solid 8 with a 7 wing, which refers to me as a Maverick. My personality is that of a risk taker who seeks out challenging new experiences in order to accomplish awe-inspiring feats. That last sentence sounds a bit over the top, and in my role as GCI President, the challenging new experiences find me more than I look for them. Mark is a 9 with an 8 wing, giving us a commonality. Maybe this commonality has been a meeting place, as well as the racquetball court.

Mark highlights the importance of accepting the love of God, not about deserving the love of God. He will have more to say in a later chapter, but please indulge me to share an observation that I believe adds to the discussion.

Coming out of the "have to" and "should" culture of legalism, it is a little hard to even allow the word "command" to pass through our ears. However, the Lord Jesus sizes up the entirety of the Bible's content in the Two Great Commandments.

One of them, an expert in the law, tested him with this question: "Teacher, which is the greatest commandment in the Law?" Jesus replied: "'Love the Lord your God with all your heart and with all your soul and with all your mind.' This is the first and greatest commandment. And the second is like it: 'Love your neighbor as yourself.' All the Law and the Prophets hang on these two commandments." (Matthew 22:35-40 NIV)

So, I should whole-heartedly love God and love my neighbor as I love myself. To quote Dr. Phil – "How's that working for you?" We're back to Paul's dilemma he eloquently described in Romans 7, knowing good and doing good. These don't always line up so well. Just like Paul, we thank God that through Jesus we can be delivered. Here is the key: Unless we first accept the Triune God's unconditional love for us, we do not have the love to give – either back to God or to our neighbor.

It is his love that liberates us, empowers us and allows us to join him in his transformative work for all humans. Thank you, Jesus!

Reflection Questions

- Who do you perceive God to be, even alongside your sins, sufferings, and feelings about yourself?
- What is the personality and nature of the one who hears your prayers?
- How strongly do you identify with what Paul says about his personal condition in Romans 7 (you may want to read the chapter)?
- How has accepting and receiving God's unconditional love transformed you?

Chapter 9 – Mark

What if Jesus Understands our Fear, Anger and Depression?

I have said this to you, so that in me you may have peace. In the world you face persecution. But take courage; I have conquered the world!
John 16:33 NRSVA

GREG AND I HAVE GIVEN personal and biblical examples of individuals who became angry, afraid, or depressed. You know what I find interesting? I don't know anyone who naturally likes any of those emotions. I do know people who are thrill seekers, people who do risky things for a rush and say, "It was scary," but that's not the kind of fear I'm talking about. I'm talking about the kind of fear that makes you feel like you are going to die, or makes you want to die. The kind of fear that makes you want to get in your car, slam it in gear, floor it, speed away as fast as you can, and never turn back. Some have been fortunate to be able to run from things that have made them experience this level of fear; most don't get that chance. Most need to learn to cope with it in one way or another. And that is where the emotions anger and depression come into the picture.

I think we have all experienced this level of fear; I'm not sure we all are aware of it or would know how to talk about it, because coping with it often becomes what one considers their normal. So, it may mean the fear that was experienced is unresolved. And if that is the case, one has yet to reconcile with the source of the fear.

So, what exactly am I saying? Do I mean you can never be happy? No, that's not what I mean. Do I mean that we will always be in a pit of despair our entire lives until we die or Jesus returns? No, that's not what I mean either. What I do mean is that sometimes life will seem very hard, and coping with those times means that you may have to live with and through the hard times, with the desire for heaven still being in your heart. And that, my friends, is the paradox. God created us with the desire to be in heaven; the trust that must develop to believe in that plan is the part of the process of life.

In the first three chapters of Genesis, we see how God is going to relate to all of creation until his kingdom is completely established in a manner where we can be in his presence for eternity. Let me explain.

In my opinion, Eve just didn't walk up to the tree out of mere impulse and decide to pick the fruit. Think about it. These two have been living together in "heaven on earth," and they had the presence of God at their beck and call. So, if they were living in such a wonderful environment, why pick that fruit from that tree? Aside from the fact that human nature always wants what it cannot have, and this was the only tree they were told to avoid, let me take a different approach.

Most of us make the assumptive mistake that this incident happened soon after they were created, but what if that's not the case? What if they have been in the garden for years? What if they have been relating to God and to each other for quite some time? What would that be like for them?

Believe it or not we can all answer that question. How long they were in the garden is irrelevant. Weeks, months, years, doesn't really matter. Think of your experiences. You're with someone for a while and what happens? Maybe they say something that hits you a little off. Maybe you felt like they were cruel, or curt, or mean, or even selfish. What do you do? How do you respond? Well, depending on your personality and conflict management approach, that may vary. So, let's think about Adam and Eve; they were human, so it was only a matter of time before they hurt one another's feelings. Did they "talk it out"? Did they completely resolve the issue and reconcile? Probably not. How do we know this? Because, somewhere along the line, Eve thought and felt that if she could "learn" more, something in their experience might improve. How do we know this? Because it's the tree of the "*knowledge* of good and evil," not the tree of "good and evil." So, remember the phrases at the beginning of the book: "you don't know, and you don't know that you don't know." And the second phrase: "your response to a 'crisis' is more important than the 'crisis' itself." Well, the first humans who had the chance to experience those phrases as reality were none other than – you guessed it – Adam and Eve.

To make a long story short, Eve walks up to the tree and scripture states that Adam was with her; she turns and hands the fruit to him after she eats. Why didn't he stop her? Why did she go there in the first place? The answer is they felt that what they had wasn't enough. And the serpent capitalizes on this perception. Because that's what it was, a perception. Based on what? Their experience. But what had they experienced? If I know husbands and wives the way I think I do, they had experienced the reality that they did not agree on everything, let alone get along all the time. So, what was their answer? We have to learn how to "fix" this problem. And, in my opinion, that is why they find themselves in front of the only tree they were instructed not to partake of. The result was catastrophic. They ran from God when they heard him walking through the garden calling for them. And when they finally did answer, they said they heard God coming and were…you guessed it…AFRAID. So, God asked them if they had eaten from the tree, and you know the rest of the story. Eve blamed the serpent, Adam blamed Eve, and then eventually blamed God for creating her in the first place. Yes, my friends, fear and anger…but what about the depressed part?

Remember, there is a short phrase in their answer to God calling them. They said they were afraid, but they also said they realized they were naked. What does that have to do with anything? Well, being naked has to do with being ashamed with what they now perceived they were. This shame came because of knowing good from evil. They had just broken the only rule they had been given. But it is so much more than that. They made the decision to DEPEND on what they thought was the right thing to do in their minds. They wanted more "knowledge." In other words, relating with God personally was not enough…they wanted to "know" more. And when they decided to depend on gaining more knowledge with the anticipation of changing things for the better, they had to live with the fact that they had depended on their own thoughts and ideas, not God's. So, the shame that came from not being able to cope and overcome the knowledge of good and evil led them to the only reasonable conclusion in their minds.

Not only was what they did bad, it progressed to them believing that what they ARE is bad. And fear and shame became their primary motivators. They blamed one another and then blamed God. They were now defensive, not collaborative and trusting. And that, my friends, can make you feel like you are out of control. And this can lead to depression.

Let me tell you a story to prove my point. The story of Tamara; otherwise known by her friends as "TK."

When TK was born, for some reason the doctor in charge did not realize that she was not getting enough oxygen. It was the late '50s, and this was a very small rural hospital. So, all the parents could do is hope for the best. As time passed, it became quite evident that TK was physically delayed in her development. She didn't learn to walk until she was almost three. And that was only possible with the aid of custom fit leg braces that she had to wear for several years. Later, it was evident to all the other children that TK could not walk like everyone else. In fact, she couldn't really run. So, she was eventually diagnosed with mild to moderate Cerebral Palsy.

In the fourth grade, when others began to write short stories, TK still could not write legibly, so it was decided that she could possibly learn to type. And in fact, she did learn to type. The problem was, she sat at the edge of all her classes by herself typing away, trying to keep up, as the other children watched and made fun of the girl with the typewriter who could barely walk, and was too ashamed to try to run. Despite all this, TK worked hard in school and got excellent grades. It was TK's hope that this would take away some of the ridicule; it didn't. In fact, it backfired in many ways. Because the "girl with the typewriter" was doing better than most of the others, and that did not go over well. When TK became a teenager, she was quite cute, in many ways attractive. Despite her awkward walk, she had a cute figure and was kind to all, despite the ridicule. And then something happened. TK discovered alcohol. By the time she was fourteen years old, as she told the story, the only thing she was anticipating was getting something to drink; it allowed her to mask the deep, dark pain. And it allowed her to be accepted by people who did not give her attention otherwise.

Decades later, TK would tell me that, in hindsight, she considered herself a full-blown alcoholic when she was fourteen years old. As she progressed through high school, she continued to get good grades, but she also began to get in trouble. She was in several car wrecks – some were quite serious. Miraculously, she wasn't driving, and she wasn't hurt. She would later say the reason she wasn't hurt was because she was always drunk.

She went on to graduate high school and get a college degree. She became an adult special needs case worker...no surprise there. During this time, she met a man who introduced her to marijuana. So now, TK had another vice. And from that point on, things only got worse. TK's first marriage did not last, and by the time she divorced, her need for "vices" was burned into her reality. She was eventually married again. But of course, her second husband had the same vices. And eventually those vices took the life of TK's second husband.

As she told her story, she said his death was too much to bear and that's when she went off the "deep end." She started expanding her vices and was eventually fired and stripped of all her licenses and certifications because she was stealing from her special needs clients to feed her habit. During this time of shame, loss, grief, depression and anger, TK was introduced to her most dangerous vice, meth.

For the next three years, TK lived for meth. She became involved with a group that was manufacturing a lot of the meth for the central part of the US. During this time, she had become an emaciated eighty-three-pound walking skeleton.

A turning point in TK's life started one early morning at three am, when her huge four-door Cadillac was being used to move the main parts of the meth lab. The driver crossed the lane just enough to catch the attention of the only oncoming car on a desolate two-lane highway in central Kansas. In the other car was a sheriff. He immediately whipped his car around, turned on his lights and chased down TK and the man who was with her – the main guy in charge of the meth lab.

As TK told the story, she felt a tremendous "heat" in her soul when that sheriff turned on his lights. You see when this happened, TK was fifty years old and had been involved with addictive level alcohol and drug use for more than thirty-five years. She would tell many of us later that she knew the "heat" she felt inside of her was God. She also knew she was done for. This would be her third strike, and she was going to prison for a very long time.

TK was forced to sober up from meth in an isolation cell. She was continually watched over by a nurse. Even so, she was offered no other drugs to help with the withdrawal. They would check her vitals to make sure they were acceptable, but the only thing they tried to help her with was hydration.

From that point on, TK never drank or used again. It was later told that the head of the drug ring told the authorities all they wanted to know. All his dealers, runners, financial support – everything. But there was one condition, they could not let TK go to jail; they had to go easy on her. And miraculously, the prosecutors agreed. As a result, TK was spared a mandatory seventeen-year prison sentence for felony manufacture, distribution, and sale of methamphetamine. She served five years differed adjudication, and the three felonies were never wiped from her record. This meant she could never work again. Even so, TK found a purpose; she became head over heels involved in the world of recovery – something she poured herself into until the day she died.

On a cold Thursday morning, TK got out of bed with the anticipation of experiencing her day. She dressed herself in her exercise clothes, went to the gym and was having a blast with her friends in recovery and those that knew her at the health club. And then, in the middle of an exercise class, she dropped to the floor like a rock. She had what we call the "silent killer," a brain aneurism. She didn't feel a thing, which is exactly how she wanted to die. How do I know this is what she wanted? Because one day before Christmas, TK told me and my wife that her only prayer was that if God decided to "take her," it would be painless. I heard that statement in our kitchen, as TK — my sister — visited our home for the Christmas holidays in 2021.

How does my sister's story apply to all of us who serve as leaders and pastors in churches? Tamara (that's what I always called her), is an extreme example of what is in all of us. What is it that is in all of us? It is the need to be loved. As I think of her experiences as a child, my parents did everything they could to try to make her life easier. But for some reason, in Tamara's mind and heart, it wasn't enough. Something was missing. For years, I blamed Tamara for so much of the chaos in my life. But what I didn't know and didn't know that I didn't know, was that my response to the chaos that she brought to my life was just as bad.

You see, I used religion to try to fill the emptiness in me. In principle, I became the resentful son in the prodigal son story in Luke 15. Now don't get me wrong, Tamara and I did reconcile before she died, but that doesn't mean we were both perfect, or that our relationship was picture perfect. The difference was we were both now depending on something that we simply didn't know we could depend on until we both hit our own "rock bottom."

I had become the religious, pompous know-it-all goody-two-shoes "pastor who loved everybody," not paying attention to Jesus' example as I studied to be a good pastor. If I read Jesus' life story correctly, it seems clear he would have given more time to my sister in his day than he would have me. And the reason for it had nothing to do with Jesus, but with me. I was the Pharisee that Jesus condemned. My religion had become my God. I was more concerned about "learning about God" instead of "relating with God." And when I was told that I needed help, I became resentful and angry. That eventually led to a level of depression that required medication, all because I felt like if I could just learn the right thing to do, things would get better, and God would finally give me the blessings I deserved. No!! It doesn't work that way!

If you are in a volunteer or salaried position in a church, and you're becoming angry, afraid, maybe even depressed, there is a very strong possibility that you are in denial. What I mean is that you have convinced yourself of what you think and feel should happen. You believe you know what people should do, how they should do it, when it should be done and why it should be done. "Because it's God's will, you idiots! Don't you see what I see!" Have you ever been there? I have.

If you are feeling this way or wish you could just yell this at your leadership, your congregation, or worse yet, your wife, your husband or your family, you need help…now. How do I know? Again, I've been at that place. If we're honest we all have. Why? Because in nature and spirit, we are all Adam and Eve, picking the tree of the knowledge of good and evil, thinking that if we can just get enough knowledge to do this just right, it will all be OK. It's one of the biggest lies we fall for.

I am convinced this is why so many in ministry suffer from depression. They have convinced themselves that if they just know enough, work hard enough, and do the right thing, everything will be OK. That is a lie. You and I are simply not that powerful. We need God. And our lives have been paid for by him. We are not in charge. That will either be the most encouraging thing you'll hear or the scariest. Either way, don't worry, it will be OK. It won't be easy, but these principles and processes that Greg and I are writing about are the principles that apply to life. They applied to Tamara. We must be honest about the fact that we can't do this...period. And at first, it's depressing. But then, something happens. And that's what we're going to write about in the next chapters.

Reflection Questions

- How do you relate to Adam and Eve? What lie have you fallen for?
- When was the last time you faced depression? How did Jesus help you through it?
- Tamara leaned on substance abuse, Mark leaned on religion, what are you leaning on besides Jesus?

Chapter 10 – Greg

What if We Really Are Friends of Jesus...

... participating with him in his ministry to humanity?

> *I do not call you servants any longer, because the servant does not know what the master is doing; but I have called you friends, because I have made known to you everything that I have heard from my Father.*
> *John 15:15 NRSV*

THROUGH THE COVID PANDEMIC, the pace of life changed for all of us, and especially for a hard-charging pioneer like me. It was during this time of disruption when my well thought out work calendar and plans for global travel to the multiple GCI regions was decimated. Then for a prolonged period I was not able to go to the office and like so many others, I worked from home. In my devotional time, I mused on the idea of suffering as the Apostle Paul who longed to visit the churches across Asia Minor and Europe and yet he encountered shipwrecks, delays and even imprisonment. Then in a surprising fashion I realized that Paul's prison was also a sanctuary – a place to sing songs of praise to Jesus, a place to write heartfelt letters to the churches, and a place to share the gospel message with fellow prisoners and prison guards.

The pandemic may have turned my normal mode of function upside down, but it also brought me to a new level of understanding and appreciation for my friend Jesus. During this season, I spent time on my screened-in porch and had meaningful talks with Jesus. It was amazing how he helped me to think about others, and to use the moment to send them an encouraging note and lift them up in prayer. I already mentioned this as a deeply personal time where I walked through the pages and challenges of the book *Breathing Underwater*. The Lord was using this opportunity to draw me closer to himself, and to shape me into a more patient leader who could embrace people and processes with his love and understanding. It is out of that season of growth that I was inspired to share the content of this book.

Even with the multiple stories about Jesus recorded in the gospel accounts of Matthew, Mark, Luke, and John, we only have a thumbnail sketch of his life. John remarks in his writings that if all the stories were recorded about Jesus, the world would not be able to contain the volumes. I believe this is the case because each person who encounters Jesus will have his or her unique story to tell and this multiplies by every man, woman, and child (one-hundred-plus billion stories).

We need to get a clear picture of who Jesus is. To get this focused snapshot into who Jesus is, and to see how he relates to those around him, I recommend "The Upper Room Discourse" recorded in John 13 - 17. This is a marvelous composite. (It would be time well spent if you read through these chapters – yes, I am giving you a homework assignment, and I bet you will thank me.) This long, passionate stream of communication contains profound theology that Jesus leaves with his disciples. Alongside the good theology, he shares his deep, personal thoughts of friendship and concern. In fact, Jesus is in anguish for his followers whom he calls "friends," and whom he must soon leave. His words are finely crafted to give them comfort in their present distress, and lasting meaning for their lives as they continue to grow in relationship to the soon to be ascended Lord. It is a vivid display of "place-sharing." (We'll dig deeper into this concept shortly.)

The Trinity

In John's record, Jesus eloquently articulates the relationship that he shares with Father and Spirit in the words of his prayer, *"Father, the hour has come. Glorify your Son, that your Son may glorify you"* (John 17:1 NIV). Compare this with his earlier reference when he says that the Holy Spirit *"will glorify me"* (John 16:14 NIV). Jesus paints a relational picture of how the Holy Spirit glorifies him (the Son), the Son glorifies the Father, and the Father glorifies the Son. This is the wonderful nature of the Trinity, where each member gives glory to the other. Theologians call this triune nature of God *perichoresis*. *Perichoresis* is a term that expresses perfect love and harmony, intimacy and reciprocity shared among the three persons of the Godhead.

Embracing the doctrine of the Trinity was the dramatic pivot that led to sweeping change for GCI. The story our former President, Dr. Joseph Tkach Jr. tells about our path to accepting the Trinity and his father's reaction is brilliant.

In the late 1980's, my dad received a letter from a Roman Catholic Monsignor which was quite complimentary about our former publication, *The Plain Truth* magazine. But his letter also contained a critique. He explained that he was shocked to see in our magazine, an article referring to the doctrine of the Trinity as a false pagan teaching. He asked how such a fine Christian magazine could not be aware of Church history. He emphasized that the development of the Doctrine of the Trinity was to explain to the pagans the doctrine of the Trinity, not the other way around. My dad discussed this with me and his assistant, Dr. Michael Feazell, and he decided to have Dr. Kyriakos Stavrinides, a long-time GCI Elder and currently Religion Professor at Azusa Pacific University, draft a reply.

We met with Kyriakos, who explained that he could draft a reply, but that we might be surprised to see that his reply would acknowledge that some items mentioned in the Monsignor's letter were accurate and correct. My dad asked Michael and me to study the subject and find out what was correct and what was in error. While Kyriacos was drafting the letter of reply, Michael and I would regularly meet with Kyriacos to discover what he was thinking. We were reading numerous books and articles on the doctrine of the Trinity as well.

After a few months of study, Michael and I were convinced that the one God of the Bible was indeed, Father, Son, and Holy Spirit. We wondered how we were going to break the news to my dad that our teaching had been wrong all along. Mike and I imagined that we would have to resign and leave our church jobs, or be fired and disfellowshipped. We met with my dad and told him the results and conclusion of our study and his response was, "Wow, Grandpa was right!"

My grandfather and grandmother started attending our church back in 1956 and were baptized in 1958, but there was one thing they never abandoned in their beliefs – that is the Trinity of God. They never caused division with it and did not even talk about it with anyone else but to my dad and a good friend and pastor, Dean Blackwell. They would pray every night before going to bed and finish their prayer by crossing themselves and saying amen in the name of the Father, the Son, and the Holy Spirit. To that I say, Amen! – Dr. Joseph Tkach Jr.

Jesus, as the second member of the Trinity, is eternally God to man, and man to God. He is the eternal connecting relationship, and we get to call him friend.

Place-sharing

In this same timeframe of GCI moving into orthodox Christianity, as I mentioned earlier in the book, I was connecting with Youth for Christ (an international youth ministry). I had been a schoolteacher, athletic coach, and summer camp leader. Youth ministry fit me well. So, I spent the decade between 2002 – 2012 working with Youth for Christ.

I distinctly recall attending a Youth Specialties workshop where one of the speakers made an over-the-top challenge. In his attempt to spur us on toward making new followers of Christ, he submitted the idea of us in the next life standing in front of Jesus being asked by our Lord as to why we didn't share the good news about him with every single person that we had encountered in this life. He then implied we were responsible for any of these people who may find themselves in the speaker's version of hell. This rang loudly in my ears with the sensitivity of "What am I doing for Jesus?" Certainly, he must be disappointed in me. I found the motivational speech de-motivating and quite perplexing.

As I continued to sort out this concept of evangelism and making disciples, I came upon a fresh approach from another author and speaker from the Youth Specialties circuit, Andrew Root. I found that he had the same perplexities that I held. His latest book was entitled *Revisiting Relational Youth Ministry*. I quickly devoured the book because his story was my story. Coincidental or not, I was asked to co-write a class on Trinitarian Youth Ministry for Grace Communion Seminary, and I knew that I had a primary textbook to draw from.

The central teaching that Dr. Root constantly points to is called "place-sharing." I already spoke about Jesus being the eternal link between God to man, and man to God. He is the supreme "place-sharer." He is the vicarious representative for all humanity for this age and the age to come.

The original idea of place-sharing comes from German theologian, Dietrich Bonhoeffer. He explains that as we have been transformed through Christ's vicarious action on our behalf, that through this same love we are to be "for the other." In essence, we make their infirmities our own. We meet the other in a posture of grace, taking upon ourselves deep sensitivity to their person and their needs, and all the good that is within our power we are to make theirs. The greatest good, and the greatest offering we can make to another, is to point them to Jesus (we are not the savior, he is).

In my many years of teaching, the most practical way of expressing how place-sharing is applied can be seen in the ABCs of Youth Ministry list (this list is a composite of ideas used in GCI to teach interns and camp workers). Somehow the work with young people resonates with a wide audience. I think it's the practical elements and demonstratable ways love is expressed.

ABCs of Youth Ministry

Always affirm God's love for them.

Build a relationship as if you are going to know them for the rest of your life.

Consistently be available. If young people find you're consistently unavailable, they'll look elsewhere.

Demonstrate the Gospel, along with Gospel declaration, by acts of kindness that speak their heart language.

Encourage them. You never know what the Lord will unleash with a single word of affirmation and encouragement.

Family matters (learn to see the person more and more in his/her family context). Be a partner to the parent(s).

Go wherever young people congregate. Your presence makes a difference.

Help them interpret what is going on around them in light of the interpretive key, Jesus Christ.

Invest in a few. Do for one what you want to do for everyone.

Jesus is their Lord and loves them more than you do. You don't need to solve all their problems.

Keep your word. Ask for forgiveness when you fail.

Listen sincerely (don't be leaning towards "the next thing" – they will pick up on it).

Mentoring is crucial for discipleship and leader development.

Notice their strengths and acknowledge their achievements.

Operate with appropriate boundaries.

Point to Jesus (testify to his goodness and to how he works in your life).

Quit thinking you're not cool enough to connect with youth. Be yourself...it's enough.

Remember names. ("A person's name is the sweetest sound to him in any language." – Dale Carnegie.)

Show up! And keep showing up.

Talk about what *they* are interested in without overwhelming them with questions (sprinkle in your story too).

Utilize small group ministry to engage young adults and teens. Group interaction is gold.

Vital mission process: Invite and disciple.

Wishing young people would show up at your church is not a strategy. It takes intentional relationship building.

X-pert about your neighborhood and community.

You don't need to add new appointments to your schedule. Invite them to join in what you're already doing.

Zealous in prayer for them always!

Place-sharing is friendship at the highest and deepest levels. And the more you participate with Jesus in his ministry, you discover that all ministry is relational. One of my biggest takeaways from my time in Youth for Christ was their 3-Story approach to evangelism. It is how my story and my friend's story intersect, and then how our stories are permeated and overshadowed by the meta-narrative of God's story. The Triune God is the "Great Connector" bringing all his children to glory.

Divine Participation

The central teaching and prioritizing of personal, meaningful, deep relationships cannot be missed in Christ's teachings. Jesus tells these original followers, "I no longer call you servants...but friends." They still understood that he is Lord and Master, and yet the Lord and Master refuses to leave them out of the good plans and activities of the Father. He is open, transparent, and inclusive. He displays true friendship and is "the true friend."

Through the presence and guidance of the Holy Spirit, Jesus will be with them, and they will carry on the same ministry he has been doing (John 14:12). The disciples/friends join this perichoretic, ever-flowing love of the Father, Son, and Spirit. This is not ethereal, or by mystical reflection on a dead hero, but by embracing the Son's mission and being empowered by the indwelling Spirit.

The call to share in Christ's love is inseparable from the call to share in Christ's labor. Let that sink in.

These disciple/friends, and all who come after, are active participants with Father, Son, and Spirit, joining their mission to the world. In GCI, it is what we call "divine participation," meaning, we do it with Jesus. In the Great Commission passage of Matthew 28, it is intentional that Christ opens his charge for the disciples to make disciples with the reality that this is done through and by his supreme authority. And then he closes the charge by assuring his followers that he is with them even into the end of the age. What a powerful, reassuring set of bookends.

What does this friendship with Jesus and shared ministry mean for me as a leader? For you as a leader? How do we actively participate? Doing ministry "with" Jesus is the key. Being the church "with" Jesus rather than being the church who does things for Jesus. Allow me to explain.

In the traditional evangelical church, we think of evangelism, discipleship, and worship as being the primary components of what we do, and certainly these are good practices. However, we can easily take these upon our shoulders and get caught up in what we are doing "for" Jesus and inadvertently move Jesus from center stage to backstage. In the western world in particular, it is so easy to measure ourselves in what we have produced, earned, and built. To discover the goodness of Jesus, our total reliance upon him, and then to rest in him moving in the rhythms of intimate relationship, is the true calling of our friend

Jesus. This is the "secret sauce" being missed in the wide range of those who identify themselves as Christian.

Faith, Hope and Love

In GCI we have not ignored evangelism, discipleship, and worship, however we have reframed the way we define and approach the work of the church. We see evangelism through the virtue of love. We see discipleship through the virtue of faith. And we see worship through the virtue of hope. The weakness of evangelism, discipleship, and worship is that it can be seen as originating with us the believers and flowing back to God. The supremacy of faith, hope and love is that it originates in the person of Jesus. It is who he is, his nature and the very fabric of his ministry to humanity.

In a visit to the island nation of Trinidad-Tobago, I had the good pleasure to share lunch with Pastor Derek Davis and his wife Elanor. Derek is a pastor's pastor and a keen learner. He picked my brain with stimulating questions from "What books am I reading?" to "How do we be a healthy GCI church within our cultural setting?" Then the *piece de ré·sis·tance* question, "Why are we defining the church's work with faith, hope and love?"

Before the "why" question can get a sufficient answer, we must begin with the "who" question. And the supreme who of all who is the Triune God revealed in the person of Jesus. It is Jesus who is Creator, Savior and King. There are no better words or concepts to describe Jesus than faith, hope and love, and consequently the ministries that flow out from his church will be a vivid expression of the faith, hope and love that is Jesus.

Why is faith, hope and love so profound for our church? I truly believe that we are following the lead of the Holy Spirit. In conjunction, we also follow the lead of the Apostle Paul and the early New Testament church, who followed the lead of the Holy Spirit. Let's look at some of Paul's writings.

In the middle of their varied disorders and factions, Paul reminds the church leaders and members at Corinth of the high value and absolute necessity of faith, hope and love. He refers to them as the greatest virtues that speak to who Jesus is and what he is about in his active ministry to humanity.

For now we see in a mirror indirectly, but then we will see face to face. Now I know in part, but then I will know fully, just as I have been fully known. And now these three remain: faith, hope and love. But the greatest of these is love. (1 Corinthians 13:12-13 NET)

Chapter 13 of 1 Corinthians is the capstone to important teaching concerning spiritual gifts and godly living (chapters 12-14). Paul articulated the diversity of gifts available to believers as the Spirit orchestrates, and then emphasized the necessity of maintaining unity among themselves under the virtues of faith, hope and love. The successful use of spiritual gifts by and among believers must be undergirded by faith, hope and love.

So, is faith, hope and love an isolated topic trapped in 1 Corinthians 13? Not at all. Faith, hope, and love are indeed prominent in the Scriptures. Let's look at a few examples.

We heard about your faith in Christ Jesus and the love that you have for all the saints. Your faith and love have arisen from the hope laid up for you in heaven, which you have heard about in the message of truth, the gospel that has come to you. (Colossians 1:4-6a NET)

Here in Colossians, we see that hope has a vital connection with faith and love. All three work together to provide "a confident hope" for the believer, which not only assures of a heavenly, eternal future, but empowers the believer to live a godly life here and now.

To believers in Thessalonica, Paul picks up with the "Big Three" as he tells the church:

We must stay sober by putting on the breastplate of faith and love and as a helmet our hope for salvation. For God did not destine us for wrath but for gaining salvation through our Lord Jesus Christ. He died for us so that whether we are alert or asleep we will come to life together with him. (1 Thessalonians 5:8-10 NET)

Faith and hope are grouped together at the opening of the "Hall of Fame" faith chapter in the book of Hebrews (Hebrews 11). This chapter speaks to a wide range of people in a wide range of circumstances, and it shows how through Jesus the believer can live a settled life in an unsettled situation. And how living in a threatening, chaotic world, there can be an active and confident faith in God, and the believer can live a life of assured hope. For all "Pilgrims" to come, this end is what Jesus, and his church is working toward.

The concepts of faith, hope and love cannot be separated from who Jesus is. It is his faith that fills my unbelief; it is his hope that covers

What if Jesus...

my doubts; it is his love that cancels my fear. And he is this Savior of perfect faith, perfect hope, and perfect love for all people. This is the personal Savior who has befriended you and me and included us in his ministry.

Faith, hope and love are the three great permanent Christian graces, as opposed to the lesser temporary gifts of prophecy, miracles, and tongues Paul speaks of in 1 Corinthians. These three "remain" and are our bedrock for ministry in GCI.

I gave mention to Pastor Derek Davis in Trinidad and his astute observations about where the Spirit is leading GCI. On a trip to Africa, I was privileged to sit through an excellent presentation by South African Regional Director, Takalani Musekwa. Takalani took the Great Commission passage of Matthew 28 and displayed very clearly how the instruction of Jesus began with the disciples worshipping him (Hope Avenue), then for them to make new disciples as they go (Love Avenue), baptizing in the name of Father, Son and Spirit and teaching all things that Christ had taught them (Faith Avenue). Takalani then took us to Acts 2 and the formation of the New Testament Church in Jerusalem. Summarizing this passage is not sufficient for the desired impact.

They devoted themselves to the apostles' teaching and to fellowship, to the breaking of bread and to prayer. Everyone was filled with awe at the many wonders and signs performed by the apostles. All the believers were together and had everything in common. They sold property and possessions to give to anyone who had need. Every day they continued to meet together in the temple courts. They broke bread in their homes and ate together with glad and sincere hearts, praising God and enjoying the favor of all the people. And the Lord added to their number daily those who were being saved. (Acts 2:42-47 NIV)

Can you see the Hope Avenue worship of prayer, communion, fellowship, and temple gathering? Can you see the Faith Avenue discipleship of learning about Jesus through the Apostles, the generous hospitality, the tangible acts of caring for one another, the growing together as the Body of Christ? Can you see the evangelism of the Love Avenue in being a bright light to their neighbors and trusting Jesus through the Spirit to add new members? Faith, hope and love are the avenues of how Jesus shares his nature with us the church, and also how he joins us with his ongoing ministry to humanity.

Leading "With" Jesus

It all starts with the Triune God. Thank you, Holy Spirit, for opening our eyes to the truth. The gospel writers give us a window into how Father, Son, and Spirit exist as three in one. I am especially drawn to how Jesus makes statements like these:

> *Very truly, I tell you, the Son can do nothing on his own, but only what he sees the Father doing; for whatever the Father does, the Son does likewise. (John 5:19 NRSV))*

> *Then he withdrew from them about a stone's throw, knelt down, and prayed, "Father, if you are willing, remove this cup from me; yet, not my will but yours be done." (Luke 22:41-42 NRSV)*

The Son does nothing apart from the Father — it is always with and through.

So, if the Son can do nothing apart from the Father, what are we able to do apart from the Son? Christian leadership begins with total dependence on Jesus and seeking his perfect will above our own. John chapter 15 gives the powerful metaphor of the vine and the branches. It is brilliant how Jesus leverages the simple biology lesson that a branch can only live and produce by being connected to the vine. He is the life-giving vine, and we are the branches. It is through his life and love that humanity has been included in the joyful mission of Father, Son, and Spirit.

It cannot be overstated that Christian ministry that produces fruit that remains will be accomplished with and through Jesus, period. When I strive to enforce my will and assert my power apart from being yielded to and relying on Jesus, it simply does not work out. Not only am I frustrated, oftentimes there is collateral damage.

One of the best illustrations I have witnessed comes from a scene in the movie *The Shack*. Jesus is interacting with the main character Mac, and he invites him to cross the lake. Rather than get in a boat Jesus grabs him by the hand and together they begin walking on water and progressing into a gleeful run across the lake. As it becomes time to return home, Mac reticently places one foot on the water's surface to test out his newly acquired skill, and his foot quickly sinks. Jesus observes his action and then simply replies, "It works better when we do it together."

Leading with Jesus means doing it together, through his power, for his perfect will, and in the joy of friendship.

Concluding Thoughts

In leadership with Jesus, it is not my role to be a "Jesus Figure," rather to be a good Jesus follower and representative. Then my responsibility is to point others to the True Vine so they too can experience an eternal friendship and an abiding home in Jesus along with the joy of producing fruit out of the shared relationship. They can use their God-given talents and resources to lead with Jesus as he guides and inspires through the Spirit.

Dane Ortlund, in his book *Gentle and Lowly*, says this:

"Here is the promise of the gospel and message of the whole Bible: In Jesus Christ, we are given a friend who will always enjoy rather than refuse our presence. This is a companion whose embrace of us does not strengthen or weaken depending on how clean or unclean, how attractive or revolting, how faithful or fickle, we presently are." (p. 115)

It thrills beyond belief to know that our Savior is our friend, and this friendship is unbreakable. Then to consider our relationship with Jesus will only grow deeper and more meaningful. Wow!

Reflection Questions

- What were the highlights for you from John's account of Jesus with his disciples in the Farewell Discourse of John 13-17?
- How have you personally experienced Jesus as friend?
- In what ways does the Faith, Hope and Love of Jesus empower you to better join Jesus in ministry to your neighbors?
- What does "Doing it with Jesus" look like for you?

Chapter 11 – Greg

What if We Are Fully Known by Jesus?

For now we see in a mirror, dimly, but then we will see face to face.
Now I know only in part; then I will know fully,
even as I have been fully known.
1 Corinthians 13:12 NRSV

FULLY KNOWN? Nothing hidden and no secrets. This sounds scary and liberating at the same time.

As Mark pointed out in Chapter 9, Adam and Eve's response to disobedience was to hide. Isn't this the common thread of the human experience? We seek recognition for our good stuff, and we want to ignore and bury the bad stuff. This game was played out in Eden and in every human setting since.

In getting to know, really know Jesus, there is an escalation of your own self-awareness. The quintessential example of this is Simon Peter.

You may recall that Peter was the one disciple who identified Jesus as the true Messiah, the Son of the living God, and Jesus told him that his Father in heaven had revealed that truth to him (Matthew 16:13-17). Moving forward in the story you will recall on the evening of the Last Supper that Peter pledged his allegiance to Jesus even unto death.

> *Then Jesus told them, "This very night you will all fall away on account of me, for it is written: 'I will strike the shepherd, and the sheep of the flock will be scattered.' But after I have risen, I will go ahead of you into Galilee."*
>
> *Peter replied, "Even if all fall away on account of you, I never will."*
>
> *"Truly I tell you," Jesus answered, "this very night, before the rooster crows, you will disown me three times."*

What if Jesus...

But Peter declared, *"Even if I have to die with you, I will never disown you."* And all the other disciples said the same. *(Matthew 26:31-35 NIV)*

The rest of the story is that after Jesus was arrested in the Garden of Gethsemane, Peter followed at a distance to the courtyard of Caiaphas the High Priest, and it was there he was confronted three times and all three times he denied Jesus. Matthew's gospel says he went outside and wept bitterly (Matthew 26:75). A statue depicting Peter's denial of Jesus is present in the same courtyard of Caiaphas today.

How much pain and sense of failure did Peter experience?

Even after Jesus was resurrected and had appeared to the disciples, Peter made the conscious decision to return to his nets. Going back to the fishing trade seemed his only option, since denying Jesus in such grand fashion was the ultimate ministry washout. It is on the beach of the Sea of Galilee where Jesus graces Peter.

The story, recorded in John 21, begins with Peter and his fishing crew of disciples deciding to return to the trade they knew before Jesus. They fish all night and come up with empty nets. Then in the early morning hours they see a figure of a man on the shore. He is yelling out to them: "Put your nets down on the other side." They had experienced this before. Peter realizing this was Jesus, covered his nakedness out of shame, then jumped into the lake to avoid confronting Jesus while he collected his thoughts. Obviously, he couldn't swim around all day, and he eventually made his way to shore. What would he say to Jesus? What would Jesus say to him?

When Peter finally comes ashore, the Lord is there to greet him and offer him food (bread and grilled fish) and then we have the record of Jesus' sweet words of restoration.

When they had finished eating, Jesus said to Simon Peter, "Simon son of John, do you love me more than these?"

"Yes, Lord," he said, "you know that I love you."

Jesus said, "Feed my lambs."

Again Jesus said, "Simon son of John, do you love me?"

He answered, "Yes, Lord, you know that I love you."

Jesus said, "Take care of my sheep."

The third time he said to him, "Simon son of John, do you love me?" Peter was hurt because Jesus asked him the third time, "Do you love me?" He said, "Lord, you know all things; you know that I love you."

Jesus said, "Feed my sheep." (John 21:15-17 NIV)

Thrice Peter denied Jesus and now thrice Jesus restores Peter. Peter is humbled by the truth that his love for Jesus is not superior to that of his fellow disciples. Do you sense the grace of Jesus in the fact that he never once talks about the three denials, and he simply reaffirms Peter's calling to care for the church that will be formed on the coming Pentecost? Peter was smarting under these three confrontations of Jesus, and yet he was simultaneously being healed and restored. Peter could finally leave his nets for good and be the "Under-Shepherd" that Jesus had made him to be.

Do you see Peter being fully known by Jesus? Can you see Peter being fully loved and fully restored in Jesus? So, how about you? Are your hidden, or even public mistakes making you hold back? Do you see Jesus' relentless pursuit of you beyond your weaknesses and self-doubt? Have you come to the place Peter did – "I'm a veteran fisherman and yet I can't catch a single fish without Jesus." It's a good place to be!

Self-awareness is Hard

Either I am a slow learner or self-awareness is just plain hard (could be both). Over the last decade I have moved from the well-known Myer's Brigg's personality types to the business personalities of The Platinum Rule to GiANT Worldwide™'s Five Voices to the ancient/modern Enneagram, and on to the LivStyle profile. I am a bit weary of self-examination. And to tell people that I am an ENTJ/ a Red-Yellow Expressive Driver/ Pioneer-Creative/ 8 with a 7 wing/ and Visionary-Instructor may not be that helpful.

My colleagues know me very well. They most frequently tag me with the Five Voice moniker of Pioneer. An episode at one of our annual leadership gatherings tells the story of how they experience me. There was a difficult issue that we had to work through in relation to our US churches. There had been previous discussion with our Regional Directors, as well as our Home Office Managers. I had spent quite a lot of time examining and praying over the matter and even gone to the extent to draft a proposal that I thought was quite good. The proposal became the focal point of our discussion. After give and take of an hour of point, counterpoint, we arrived at the place where it seemed good to the Holy Spirit and to us. The end result was different than my original proposal, but my goal wasn't that my way be "the way," but that my proposal was a starting point for discussion. The end result was the kind of process you want to happen in the life of the church.

So, after the meeting a few different leaders came up to me and thanked me, commenting on how well I had listened. I wasn't sure if I should receive their comments as intended praise or to be quasi offended. My internal view of myself is that I am a reasonable person who listens and has demonstrated this multiple times before.

The next morning after the big planning session, I was at breakfast with Michael Rasmussen (North American Superintendent) and Jeff Broadnax (Regional Director NE US). These two guys and I have experienced a lot of water over the dam and under the bridge together. Over breakfast I asked for their unvarnished truth about whether I have been a reasonable, listening leader or not. They both chuckled, and then Jeff said, "Greg, you speak fluent pioneer and so people around you hear fluent pioneer." Message received.

I was recounting this story to Michelle Fleming (GCI Communications and Media Director). I think of Michelle as one of the most introspective people I know. If you have any questions about the Enneagram personality types, she's your go to. Michelle was sharing a personal account of a fresh experience she was going through when she said, "Jesus lives in here (pointing to her heart) and I know that it is him coming out because the love, patience, and grace I'm expressing is not the normal posture of pride that comes from an Enneagram #2."

Knowing and being known by Jesus includes more than reading the historical accounts of the Bible, and it is more than hearing what other believers may share. It is exactly as Michelle so clearly articulated – it is his transforming power shaping us into his likeness. The fruit of the Spirit is overshadowing the carnal works of the flesh. In fact, the love, joy, peace, patience, kindness, generosity, faithfulness, gentleness, and self-control are replacing lust, impurity, licentiousness, idolatry, sorcery, enmities, strife, jealousy, anger, quarrels, dissensions, factions, envy, drunkenness, and carousing. Paul's theological premise of us being fully known by Jesus merges nicely with John's picture of us becoming like Jesus (1 John 3:2).

We are not talking about being absorbed into Jesus so that we disappear, rather we are progressing toward the best version of ourselves by taking on his nature. In him we move from the glory of a created child to a regenerated child living through sanctification, and onward toward becoming the glorified son or daughter. This is how Paul sums up our entire Christian life in 2 Corinthians 3:18 when he says we are being transformed into the same image from one degree of glory to another. What a marvelous progression from redemption and sanctification on earth, to our glorious eternal welcome into heaven.

Fully Known?

Nothing hidden and no secrets. I believe this makes perfect sense when Jesus said in the Sermon on the Mount that not even a sparrow falls without the attentive eye of the Triune God taking notice. As the line of the popular hymn tells us, "His eye is on the sparrow, and I know he watches me."

Romans 12 is one of those anchoring scriptures I go back to time and time again. Paul begins with this beautiful paradox that as Christ followers, we are to be "Living Sacrifices." (In the Old Testament times, animals were dead when they were placed on the sacrificial altar.) We who have received the mercies of God for salvation, and empowerment for meaningful ministry, are "living and active" as we participate with the marvelous triune God in his good, perfect, acceptable will. Transformed Christians are not mere symbols of worship, rather they are active agents of the Lord, operating through the power of the Spirit in bringing others to the reality that is Jesus.

By his grace we are enabled to see ourselves accurately, or as Paul says, "with sober judgment." We have clarity about key areas:

Alignment in relationship with the Lord Jesus and flowing in his will for us.

Seeing the ways we have been gifted by the Spirit.

Using these gifts purely and properly for the intended end of accomplishing the Lord's will and purpose.

In my sixty-plus years of living, there have been various pivotal "Aha Moments" that awakened me. Allow me to share a couple of these experiences.

In the book credits at the front, and in Chapter 2, I mention Dr. Dick Wynn. As I reflect on the challenge from Dick to be a leader of leaders, I muse on what has transpired over the past fifteen years. A significant change for me was to become intentional. Intentional means by design and with purpose. If I am who Jesus says I am, a beloved child accepted and alive in him, then it makes sense to grow in my self-awareness. How am I wired, or better yet, shaped by the Lord as I bear his image? In Dick's estimation, I am called and shaped by Jesus to be a leader, and in keeping in step with the instruction from Romans 12, I should lead to the best of my ability and for the accomplishment of the Lord's will. I can own it.

Dr. Charles Fleming, whom I refer to as my older brother from a different mother, has made many rich deposits in my life. Charles is a native Grenadian who pastored for many years and then served as the GCI Regional Director over the Caribbean Islands. Charles invited me along on a few occasions to accompany him to conferences in the islands. I always found it interesting looking at the azure blue waters and white, crystal sand from the aerial view of the plane, and then once on site remaining inside for long sessions of training and discourse (in all fairness, we did have a few occasions to dip our toes in the warm tropical ocean).

Charles is a consummate teacher and serves as adjunct professor at the prestigious Fuller Seminary in Pasadena, CA. He is a clear and innovative thinker who has dedicated his life to educating others. One of the most significant observations that he shared with me as an older brother to younger brother was how he saw me having the skill to move fluidly between the macro and micro. I am by nature a "Big Picture" person, and yet the Lord has shaped me with the ability to move in and through the weeds when necessary. This matches what I have learned via LivStyle's assessment tool, which confirmed that I am both a visionary and an instructor. If my "Big Picture" vision-casting in the style of Nehemiah doesn't work, then I will transform into the more adamant instructional style of the Apostle Peter. The challenge is to use this skill to effectively lead my team, and always to the glory of Father, Son, and Spirit.

A deeper realization that I had leadership gifting, and even specific skills that others had seen in me, was wonderfully liberating. Liberating how? In the sense that I was free and comfortable interacting with my team of leaders moving between the lofty big picture vision and the micro steps that would move us toward the vision. Knowing myself has been empowering, and it has presented opportunities to flow and connect that simply would not have happened otherwise.

Conclusion

The two key questions coming from the multi-layered story of Peter are:

Who is Jesus?

Who is Peter in Jesus?

These are questions about awareness and acceptance, questions about relationship – of knowing and being known. These questions for Peter are also questions for you, and me, and for all of God's children.

For Peter to fully appreciate that his power and purpose flowed to him from Jesus, he had to experience human weakness and human failure. The vehement, "Hell no" of not knowing Jesus over the flickering glow of the soldier's charcoal campfire, could only be rectified by a restorative conversation on the shores of Galilee by the resurrected Jesus, who cooked an inviting breakfast over the flames of a charcoal fire. And this restorative conversation didn't happen until the veteran fisherman had fished all night without catching even one fish. When Jesus the carpenter suggests trying the other side of the boat, and one hundred fifty-three fish are caught, you come to realize who is Lord. This demonstrated to Peter that even the skills he thought he could fall back on required the blessing of the resurrected Jesus. I can imagine the words from the Last Supper discourse when Jesus declares himself to be the True Vine and that we are his branches, and that apart from him we can do nothing, were words ringing in Peter's ears and soul. And they should ring in ours as well.

The correct response to being "fully known" is a surrender of self, which especially includes self-loathing or self-aggrandizement. It is through this "letting go," that we are open to interactive contact with our Creator, Savior God. Then to know Jesus more, and to wholeheartedly embrace the relationship with him, becomes the pursuit.

Jesus knows us so well that he can accurately name the number of hairs on our heads (it is an easier count for Mark – sorry, but I had to get back for his racquetball thrashings from college days). And Jesus knows way more than your anatomical makeup, he knows the depth of your heart, your desires, and your personality – and he still loves and likes you more than you can possibly imagine.

Reflection Questions

- Knowing yourself to lead yourself is paramount. How accurately would you say that you know yourself?
- Are there big brother and big sister relationships in your life who have helped you with "Aha Moments?" Can you share an example?
- What did you learn and take away from the example of Peter?
- What did you learn and take away from the example of Greg?
- What steps will you take toward further self-discovery?

- **Chapter 12 – Mark**

What if Jesus Does Accept Us Just As We Are?

For I am convinced that neither death nor life, neither angels nor demons, neither the present nor the future, nor any powers, neither height nor depth, nor anything else in all creation, will be able to separate us from the love of God that is in Christ Jesus our Lord.
Romans 8:38-39 NIV

IN CHAPTER 9, I SHARED with you a "fly over" version of my sister, Tamara's life. What I would like to share with you now is a bit more of my story. What I didn't know and didn't know that I didn't know is that my personality type exploded into life while I was experiencing the chaos of my family's reality of addiction. Unfortunately, it was not the positive loving side of my personality that was exploding. And that was something that took me decades to accept.

One Saturday afternoon in 1977, my sister and parents were in the middle of a knock-down drag-out fight. My parents were doing what most parents of addicts do, they were trying to help. What none of us knew is that it is possible to "help" a person too much. In fact, we in ministry can fall into the trap of believing that it will be our help that changes our members and congregations. That simply is not true. We are instruments of a greater truth that has the power to break through all the things that we as human beings have used to try to "fix" the pain and suffering in our lives. What is hard for church leaders to understand is this: If you give to the point of feeling like you must sacrifice your own identity and life, you are playing a role that you were never intended to play. Let me explain what I mean.

On that summer day, I made a decision that would impact me for years to come. It seemed so simple at the time, but its consequence was life changing. As my family members argued about Tamara's dishonesty and "disobedient" life, I had the following thought scream inside my head: "My family members are complete and total idiots!" The thought continued, "they don't know what the hell they are doing!" And with that, I got up from the couch, walked down the hall and went out the front door. And that moment changed me forever.

I mowed lawns that summer and raised enough money to buy a ten-speed bike. I paid more than five hundred dollars for it. Why? Because I "deserved a good bike." I then joined the local "Road Cycling" club. And of course, I was its youngest member. While my other friends were running around like teenagers normally do, I was cycling with a group of men in their forties and fifties out on the rural highways of central Kansas. What I didn't know was that after making that decision, I gave myself permission to start living by my rules. And they weren't going to be what my "idiot" family was doing – I was going to do better. And for the next thirty-plus years, unbeknownst to me, that's exactly what I tried to do.

Within the next year, I had joined what was then the Worldwide Church of God. I became the president of the youth group. I was flown to Pasadena, CA – our Home Office at the time – twice in one year for leadership opportunities...all expenses paid. I attended our denomination's private college; I became the youngest student body president in the history of the college. And when I graduated, as I previously mentioned, I wasn't hired into full time ministry. Deb and I had recently married, so I told her we were going to go to my home church, we were going to be humble, and we were going to wait for them to ask us to help...like good little Christians. And ask they did. In less than three years, I was ordained. And six months after that, I was hired into full time ministry, June 1987.

We served two and a half years in Jackson and Greenwood, MS, and almost eight years in Detroit, MI. During this time, it was discovered that we could not have children on our own and we decided to adopt. After we adopted our son, it was discovered that he had a biological sister. When she was ten months old, we adopted her too.

Our son, her biological brother, was eighteen months old when our daughter became a part of our family.

In 1995, the Worldwide Church of God changed all its major doctrines to move us more in line with mainstream Christianity. No stone was left unturned. The changes were too much for many of our local church members in Detroit, and most of them ended up leaving. During this transition, something began to happen to me personally. I began to stay in bed longer. I wouldn't return phone calls from members. I began to get irritated with Deb and the kids. I was impatient, testy, and very quick to anger. One morning, as I was getting out of bed, probably close to noon, Deb met me at our bedroom door – she had been up for several hours. She looked me straight in the eye and said, "You are a walking dead man, and I don't know what to do for you anymore." And then she turned away and walked down the stairs.

I ended up in therapy with the very therapist I was referring our members to go see. We were on such a limited income that he saw me for more than two years for free. I was diagnosed with clinical depression and ended up on 40mg of Prozac for almost five years. That medication saved my life and our marriage. In June of 1997, we were transferred to Houston, TX, where we live today.

When our children became teenagers, they began to present with some of the challenges considered normal and expected for adopted children. When that began to happen, something that had been asleep in me for years came roaring to the surface. It sounded something like this, "Oh no you don't, you're not going to act that way in my home. I've already been through this and you're not going to bring that back into my life!"

You see, I justified that response because I felt like I had sacrificed, and because of my sacrifice, no one was going to bring any more pain into my life. No matter what. In my mind, I had "survived" and made a difference when it came to the doctrinal changes in the church. Proof of that – at least to me – was that one of the sermons I had given at one of our national conferences was sent out – worldwide. But along with this "I have sacrificed attitude," came something else. I had become a cross between an enabling bumbling fool, and an angry, controlling, judgmental father and husband. I started to bring back my "old rules." The very ones that I created during the summer of 1977. But now the fuel driving those rules was a very clear and concise list of expectations. And if anyone didn't meet my expectations, I kept score. And I felt justified. Remember, I was the teenager who had survived that family of "idiots." I knew what to do. So, I believed I was going to have to "sacrifice" more to fix this mess now. What I didn't know and didn't know I didn't know, was that my response to my personal "crisis" was worse than the crisis itself. Remember the phrases I mentioned in Chapter 3? Now you understand why I need them as much as you do. It's not that I want them – I need them. Because in those phrases, I began to understand my need to ACCEPT who and what I was, even as a Christian.

I had become an angry, resentful, judgmental man, husband, and father. I was mad at the church, my kids, and my wife. Why? Because they didn't understand how hard I was trying to make all the "stuff" work! And if people would just "LISTEN!" they would understand that I know what I'm talking about. Don't they understand how much I'm sacrificing here? I was caught in a vicious circle, and this is what drove me into Al-Anon, the 12-step program for family members of addicts.

In Chapter 3 of Richard Rohr's book, *Breathing Under Water*, he discusses the third step, "Made a conscious decision to turn our will and our lives over to the care of God as we understood him" (p. 17, Franciscan Media, 2011). Rohr brings out a most humbling yet convicting idea. He states:

You see, there is a love that sincerely seeks the spiritual good of others, and there is a love that is seeking superiority, admiration, and control for itself, even and most especially by "doing good" and heroic things. Maybe we have to see it in its full-blown sick state to catch the problem.... most resentful people are very sacrificial at one level or another, the manipulative mother is invariably sacrificial, all codependents are sacrificial, a phenomenon so common that it created its own group called Al-Anon. (Ibid., p. 22)

If you are in full time ministry or are a volunteer for your church, and you are beginning to feel like no one understands how hard you are working, and you are becoming resentful because no one is understanding your sacrifice, forgive the phrase but... "Houston, we have a problem."

I don't mean to trivialize the reality, but we all must be honest about how we're feeling about our responsibilities, and what we may be expecting in return.

What if Jesus...

There was a time when I was first in Al-Anon, that one of the people I thought I needed to "help" had a big setback. I was mad! I called another LPC that was working with this group. When she picked up the phone, I lost it. After about one minute, she interrupted me and yelled, "ARE YOU DONE!!" I answered her with a few choice words that would make most Christian's ears melt off, and her reply was the following: "Get your __s off the cross, we need the firewood!" That phrase shut me down. I was putting myself on the cross and taking Jesus down – as if me on a cross has any value. Her point was clear – my cross has no value, except perhaps firewood.

I realized that it was my expectations that had become my "gods." They were the things that I had created back in the summer of 1977 to give me a purpose to keep going. (The concept of falling back into this pattern was as simple as "riding a bike.") When I didn't meet those expectations, I had a reason to try harder. When others didn't meet them, I had a reason to "sacrifice and love them more...to help or fix them." It was all a lie. And I didn't know that I didn't know. My rock bottom was realizing that the rules that my family had created to justify their fighting and arguing with the intentions to help and be heard, were nothing compared to the rules that I had created to survive what I felt was my suffering.

I had become what I hated.

And that, my friends and church leaders, is the core of acceptance. No matter how many rules you create, no matter how much you love someone or something, you do not have the power to change any person, let alone save them. In fact, if you honestly come to the point of this realization, you will begin to comprehend why Paul wrote, "for your sakes, we die daily." Because that is what it feels like. And Jesus told us it would be this way. In John 16:33, he basically stated in this life we would "suffer," but then he told us not to lose heart, he had overcome the world. Notice, he doesn't say he will give us the power to overcome the world – he did it *for* us.

Can you accept that?

Every morning of every day of my life, I must ask God for the strength to "accept" this reality of the gospel. It is God who saves through perfect love, not me.

So, you may be saying, "Then why in the world would I stay in the church or in ministry? This sucks!" Here's a small truth: we're no longer talking just about ministry – now we're talking about life. You can leave ministry. And, if you feel like it is honestly not the job for you, I encourage you to do so. But if you choose to leave, you better be honest about what you are expecting out of life. You may be leaving what you think is the source of your problems, but if you take those expectations with you, it's only a matter of time before you will have the same feelings and experiences elsewhere. The context and people and job may be different, but because of your expectations, you will once again be looking for a change because you will be feeling like no one understands how hard you work and how much you care. And if you expect a new job or town, or a new wife, or a new whatever it is you think will make your life better, then there's a pretty good chance that the thing you have yet to accept is yourself.

Now, after you've walked across the room and picked the book off the floor because you just got mad at me and threw it, remember this, God loves you unconditionally, despite the rules and expectations he knows you've been hanging on to for years. Yes, grace truly is amazing.

In the book *Addiction and Grace*, Gerald May, M.D. expresses this idea by saying this:

Thus ironically, we must have attachments (those were my expectations) if we're to be free. We have to turn away before we can come home with dignity. Just as God invites us toward love, we must be pulled away. Just as we crave freedom, we must be seduced into slavery. It is here, perhaps, that temptation begins to make a little sense in the light of love. It is still not an attractive concept; I do not think it was ever meant to be. Our temptations are trials, certainly. And each of our addictions (mine was my ideas, feelings and thoughts) proves how we have responded—not simply from our conscious will, but from the totality of our being. In a sense, then, temptations are trials and tests of who we are as complete human beings. But they are trials and tests for our own growth, not for God to find out how good we are. (*Addiction and Grace*, Gerald May, Harper Collins, 1991, Pg. 117).

I had to accept that when I began to feel like no one understood how much I cared, and how hard I was trying, I was figuratively hanging myself on the cross and taking Jesus down. My "addictions" had become expecting people to understand me, encourage me, praise me. The problem was, I didn't trust anyone enough to tell them how I was feeling. Remember my rules. When I judged everyone as "idiots," my subconscious rule became "you have to do this on your own, you can't trust anyone...they won't understand how much it hurts." What I didn't know is that my pain had isolated me from the closest ones that loved me, and I had no idea what to do, what to say, or how to act. It was scary, it made me mad, I resented it beyond words...it was my "rock bottom." I had to accept that I was powerless and to begin to trust that in the middle of the overwhelming unspeakable sense of being totally out of control and scared, God was with me in a manner that I had yet to understand, let alone accept.

Acceptance begins when you begin to realize that your pain in life is not a curse because you did something wrong. Pain is the avenue that you can travel to find God. He is the only one that can bear the depth of that pain with you at an intimate, gut level. But you first have to accept that it's there. He never promised to remove the pain from us, but he did promise that he would be in it with us, and he would give us a strength that we do not have in order to bear it. And in some weird, paradoxical way, that reality is freeing.

Greg used the illustration of Paul and his "thorn in the flesh" in Chapter 4. Three times Paul pleaded to God to remove this "thorn in the flesh." Whatever the "thorn" was, it seemed to be causing unbearable, emotional, psychological, and spiritual disillusionment and pain. God didn't remove the thorn, but he gave us that powerful statement: "My grace is sufficient for you."

We have to consider that this was not a corrective statement that was meant to put the Apostle Paul in his place; it was a statement of fact that was presented to Paul. So, the variable in coping with and experiencing our pain is not whether God is there or not. The variable is whether we can accept that what God has already done for us in the birth, life, death, resurrection, and ascension of Jesus is enough. The choice will always be ours to accept.

Reflection Questions

- Have you recognized patterns of unhealthy relating that you experienced in your family of origin?
- Like Mark came to see, his personal rules and expectations were his greatest hindrance to intimacy with God and others. What hinders you?
- How has your personal experience with pain and suffering been an avenue to bring you closer to Jesus?

- As you look over your personal life experiences and emotions, where can you join with the Apostle Paul and collectively say, "His grace is sufficient?"

Chapter 13 – Greg

What if Jesus is Present With Us Even to the End of the Age?

Now the eleven disciples went to Galilee, to the mountain to which Jesus had directed them. When they saw him, they worshipped him; but some doubted. And Jesus came and said to them, "All authority in heaven and on earth has been given to me. Go therefore and make disciples of all nations, baptizing them in the name of the Father and of the Son and of the Holy Spirit, and teaching them to obey everything that I have commanded you. And remember, I am with you always, to the end of the age."
Matthew 28:16-20 NRSVA

IN THIS CHAPTER YOU WILL SEE me circle back to ministry (that's what pioneers do).

Have you heard of GC² ministry? It's the powerful combination of Great Command and Great Commission ministry. For many years in GCI, we've talked about loving God and people, and about being disciples who make disciples. Any church that is Bible-based should get this.

And it is true, many other churches teach and believe in GC² ministry. Eric Burtness, a Lutheran pastor and consultant, says this about his book to the Lutherans:

"That's what this book is about. As each chapter unfolds, you'll see specific ways in which your congregation can develop Great Commandment and Great Commission ministries that can transform your congregation's ministry to celebrate God's presence in worship, demonstrate God's love through ministry, communicate God's Word through evangelism, incorporate God's family through fellowship and educate God's people through discipleship." (Introduction from *Leading on Purpose*)

So, what if these good efforts that we label as worship, ministry, evangelism, fellowship, and discipleship fall short? What if they simply become containers for human effort? Even if the various programs are wonderfully designed, and the people who oversee and operate these endeavors are talented and dedicated, there is no guarantee that the church is being the church.

The instructional words of the glorified Jesus to the remaining eleven disciples (who were now Apostles), were not so much about "how-to" as it was about "who-through." The passage begins with the followers worshipping Jesus (the Hope Avenue). Then Jesus provides wonderful bookends to his life-giving words. First, he proclaims that ALL authority in heaven and earth is his, therefore our operations are under his direction and by his power. His closing declares that he will remain present in his people and his church even to the end of the human age. Earlier in Matthew's writing Jesus assured these same guys by announcing his intention of building "his church" with the promise that the gates of hell would never prevail (Matthew 16:17-19). Can we get any better guarantees than the definitive words of our Savior and King?

There is even more comfort in the Matthew 28 passage as Jesus tells us that, "as we go," we should freely share his love and talk openly about him and his saving grace (sounds like the Love Avenue). As people are drawn to Jesus and his good news, they celebrate this relationship in the waters of baptism. And they aren't joined to any sect or social club, they are joined in relationship to the Holy Trinity – Father, Son, and Spirit. Then the church continues to guide new believers to the teachings and values of Jesus. Growing in relationship with the Triune God and in the community of the church is this "New life in Christ!" (Did I hear a GCI leader say, "This is the Faith Avenue"?)

Do you get the picture? It isn't you or me alone in our limited efforts to make Christian disciples. Ultimately, we are junior partners who join with the Lord of the universe, who in his mysterious way is drawing all of humanity to himself – even when it appears the whole world is headlong in the opposite direction. This is one of the great paradoxical mysteries of the God revealed in Jesus.

Jesus prefaces his promise of remaining present with a powerful statement – "And remember." Other translations say, "Surely," or "And behold...," which are definitive statements. Why the reminder? Two things. We as humans are easily distracted, and with the loud noise and strong pulls of this 21st century world, we can forget who Jesus is and what he is up to. The second thing is our hubris. Somehow, we start believing that we are independently good enough, smart enough, and then we want to take credit. This is where surrender plays such a pivotal role (enter the Great Command).

It is loving God with our hearts, minds, and souls that creates the space for surrender. This surrender means no longer acting as lord of my own life, captain of my own ship, or master of my fate. Rather, I give my life to Jesus in humble submission and complete dependence on him. This is not just an easy exchange with an onward, upward trajectory (I think this point has been loud and clear throughout the book). It is a day-to-day journey with ups and downs, and some sideways experiences. What I have discovered in my sixty-plus years is that he is faithful and constant when I am unfaithful and fickle, and his promise to never leave or forsake me is sure. It reminds me of a senior co-worker at his retirement party who said, "If I had been supervising me, I would've fired myself a long time ago." And just think, in our human frailty we give Jesus "just cause" to fire us, but that's not who he is.

Surrendering takes vigilant attention on my part (even though Jesus remains Lord whether I submit or not). I must be awake, alert, and aware if I am to actively participate in the good things Jesus is doing in me and around me. My salvation is not linked to my attentiveness – that would be salvation by works. However, the depth of my relationship with Jesus and my personal growth are very much linked to being aware of his presence and Lordship. I've heard it said that everybody gives their devotion and attention to some cause or activity, and in essence, we all have an object of worship. Where does Jesus rank in my life and yours?

A small example of where I experience surrender is in the singing of songs and hymns with good theology, and especially when they are sung within the chorus of other believers (a great dearth in my life during the COVID pandemic). One of the best examples is John

Wyeth's *Come Thou Fount of Every Blessing (tune my heart to sing thy praise)*. Every stanza is deep with meaning, and the final verse pricks my heart every time.

O to grace how great a debtor daily I'm constrained to be!
Let thy goodness, like a fetter, bind my wandering heart to Thee.
Prone to wander, Lord, I feel it, prone to leave the God I love;
Here's my heart, O take and seal it, seal it for thy courts above.

The action of surrender to the Lord's presence in our lives and in our world is ultimately worship. It is throwing down every personal trophy, all degrees, and all titles. I recall Paul calling these earthly accomplishments rubbish, and the Greek etymology of the word indicates excrement, feces, dung. For Paul, all his energy exerted toward human achievement was replaced by the burning passion of knowing Jesus. Really, really knowing Jesus, even in the experience of suffering and in the power of the resurrection. This is the depth that Mark and I are continually seeking, and in this book have been pointing toward.

Our Need for the Church

Because of his abiding presence and constant attention, Christ's profound promise that the gates of hell will not prevail against the church through the ages of human history is a true saying. Not because human church leaders are so great, smart, or faithful, but because Jesus is faithful to be the head of his church through all ups and downs on all continents, until the Father gives the Son the word for his return.

Jesus is so in tune with our human frailties that he gave us the church to be our spiritual mother. The Body of believers nurtures us, includes us, and attends to our spiritual growth. Throughout this book we have shown our undeniable reliance on Jesus, and as we need Jesus, we also need his church. I pray that GCI never loses its high value on ecclesiology (the significance of the church in the world and in people's lives).

Earlier we expressed how we participate with Jesus in his ongoing mission of drawing all humanity to himself, and this drawing includes life within the community of other believers. Foremost in the church, godly unconditional love should be experienced – you are loved simply because you are a child of God. Consider what Jesus communicated to his original followers in John 13:35, *"By this everyone will know that you are my disciples, if you have love for one another"* (NRSV). The receptive, inclusive love of Jesus should be present and felt.

It is within the flow of daily life and interaction with other believers where we discover how and where we fit. Through accurate self-discovery and self-awareness we find our "best fit" placement in the church. When we fit well, we experience heightened significance and purpose. Paul told the Corinthians that God the Holy Spirit places every member in the body as he has chosen. This is what we hope for and aspire to, spiritual appointments for church offices and positions of service.

There is an age-old question about whether leaders are born or leaders are made. The answer is yes and yes, and for the sake of the church, the question about the calling and the appointment of the Holy Spirit looms even larger. It is within the community of believers at the local church level, that fruits of calling to church offices will be recognized and validated. In GCI's governance system, the application process requires approval from regional supervisors and then ultimately comes to my desk at the Home Office for the final review. We continue to learn as we work through this process, and I am proud of how GCI is vigilant about the recognition and appointment of church elders.

It is within a loving, Christ-centered church, where we learn the art of "one-anothering." There are some fifty-nine Bible verses that speak to one-anothering. The list speaks of responsibilities we have to one another. Responsibilities like encouraging, exhorting (truth-telling in love), honoring, being at peace, bearing one another's burdens (like holding up one end of a heavy couch), loving, and on and on. This is the kind of community where the presence of Jesus is palpable.

Our denominational vision for GCI is Healthy Church. And succinctly put, Healthy Church is church where Christ is Lord and his love experienced. If this is clearly understood and experienced by everyone who partakes in a GCI church service or activity, that will mean our vision is being realized. Not an achievement, but rather a state of being, and a state that requires attention and maintenance.

Because of Christ's Abiding Presence

Because of Christ's presence, the GC^2 ministry referred to by Burtness is fitting. Keep in mind that Burtness' idea originates in the words and teachings of Jesus.

The Great Command recorded in Matthew 22:34-40 instructs us to have a whole-hearted yearning for God, and the New Testament writers follow this us up with an unwavering dependency on Jesus and identity found only in relationship to him. The second part of the Great Command is to have sacrificial, unconditional love for people. Paul adds to this when he says that we are not to look at any person in a human way, rather we are to see all people under the grace and spilled blood of Jesus.

Jesus says that all the law and prophets hang on these two commands. Outward love toward God and people are the grounding anchors of the Christian faith.

GC² ministry works when we remember that it is about "who through" before the "how to." What a privilege to work with and through Jesus, under his authority and for the good of the eternal kingdom.

Society's View of the Church

You may recall Ned Flanders from the nineties. The obtuse neighbor of *The Simpsons* was a predictable stereotype of Christians – at least as it stood thirty years ago. He's Magoo, innocent and obnoxiously benign, seen always wearing the same sweater and memorizing scripture for fun.

But does Ned still apply today? Has the perception of the church changed much since Ned first declared, "Okilly dokilly?"

His stereotype still gets some things right perhaps. The perception of Christians – especially the evangelical brand – as credulous and out-of-touch, still stands. We are perceived as irrelevant to the culture because we are withdrawn from it, safe within our circled wagons.

Like Ned, we're thought of as judgmental and standoffish, unwilling to be sullied by "the world" and its moral tarnish. We develop our own music, novels and even video games to keep the margins wide between "us" and "them."

When confronted with a stereotype like this, we forget the arguably good parts of it. Ned was at least a safe character. His dull life was a neutralizing contrast to the Simpson family turbulence. He had a stable marriage and odd, but happy children. He was also not a hypocrite – Ned was who he said he was.

It's this part that might be under fire in recent history. Ned Flanders has taken on a rough edge of late. He's not only become out of date; he's known more for what he stands against. He's not just annoying, he's becoming threatening and potentially violent.

Anxiety, extremism, and media frenzy have recreated the Flanders stereotype into something more dangerous and less trustworthy.

In recent years, white evangelicalism and radical nationalism became almost synonymous in the headlines (whether totally accurate or not). Obstinate church gatherings despite COVID warnings became a media darling. The Ned Flanders caricature was redrawn with only the sharp angles.

We look like hypocrites who claim to be running by different rules, but in the end are just as bullying and contrived as anyone else. Out of touch, bland, credulous, irrelevant, but now added to that list is angry and possibly even dangerous. Perhaps these are unfair stereotypes of us as Christians, but they're alive and cannot be ignored.

Through deep self-reflection and honest evaluation, some larger church movements in the US have admitted their shortcomings. The well-known Willow Creek Church said this, *"We failed. We baptized some people, but they're not actually maturing."* What honesty. Willow Creek's humble submission resonates with me and other leaders in GCI. Willow Creek's founder moved forward into another set of personal problems, but still they got this one right about the need to attend to the "Faith Avenue" of ministry, helping new believers grow in their relationship to Jesus and within the family of faith.

The great challenge to the church of the 21st century is to overcome the negative stereotype and be known by how we live our lives relationship by relationship – in family, neighborhood, workplace and beyond. This turnaround can only come through the power and presence of Jesus in our lives with his transforming love! We are back to the "who through." And it is through Jesus, and Jesus only, that Christianity can be transformed into the inviting, alluring, positive and life-giving organism it is intended to be.

The church must move beyond the inward Starbuck lounge, social club mentality, and retake ownership of its mission to make genuine followers of Jesus. Paul would tell us that believers need to move beyond their infancy and continue to grow into maturity, which means deeper relationship with Jesus and becoming more like him. The church must foster such an environment that maturation in Christ is happening. We cannot attach the church to political leaders, movements, or ideologies. There is one leader – Jesus. It is his movement, his ideology, his mission, which brings glory to the Father. It is his kingdom we seek.

For my younger proteges (for whom this book is written), I would suggest that the condition of the church and how it is being viewed by society will be the greatest challenge of your lives. But take heart, Jesus is intimately, personally in the challenge with you and you with him.

Conclusion

During the COVID-19 pandemic, my life was re-arranged (yours too, I bet). As President of GCI, I was accustomed to flying around the world and working with and through our international church leaders. The first book I wrote was almost entirely written from the seat of a plane flying over some ocean or foreign continent. The virus totally grounded me, and to add insult to injury, it made me stay home and use my dining room table for my office desk (where I am writing from right now).

Early on during this adjustment period, Mark had recommended that I read Richard Rohr's book *Breathing Underwater*. He said that it would help me to better understand him. So, for a couple of months this book became more than just another informative book, it became my daily devotional. And perhaps I did learn a thing or two about Mark, but surprisingly I was discovering more about myself, and my resolute need for Jesus. It was my wake-up call to what the Lord is doing in me.

Rohr repetitively uses the word "radical." Radical is appropriate because the weight of our relationship with Jesus is beyond mild and casual. I shall list a few of his statements that jarred me into the realness of my life with Christ.

"A radical surrendering of our will to Another whom we trust more than ourselves." (p. 21)

The Challenge – Trust more than myself?

"We have been graced for a truly sweet surrender, if we can radically accept being radically accepted – for nothing!" (p. 27)

The Challenge – Accept being accepted?

"The only way to be delivered from our 'body of death' is a love that is greater, a deeper connection that absorbs all the negativity and irritation with life and with ourselves." (p. 113)

The Challenge – A love that absorbs all the negativity and irritation?

Don't these statements stop you in your tracks? We discover that Jesus is not merely the object of our trust, he is a deeply personal God who is trustworthy. This catapults us into closer relationship. He meets us even in our powerlessness, failures, and indignities. Unfortunately, much of Christianity would paint this scenario as God distancing himself and shunning us in our pool of brokenness and sinfulness, rather than meeting us.

Surrender is not merely about giving up. It is more about acceptance – accepting that Jesus loves you, me and the other. He accepts because you, me and the other are his beloved individual children, period. Accepting and receiving is hard for us, especially when we live in a world that says you must perform and earn.

Within the communion and daily conversations with Jesus, deep appreciation and gratefulness spring forth in surprising ways. For me, the resentment of having people whom I perceived at odds with me (or in the worst circumstances, enemies), dissipated as my connection and reliance on Jesus deepened. Let me explain further. As a pioneer, it has been most difficult for me to work through the people who oppose my "good ideas," or bring what I perceive to be negativity to the group, or painfully slow down processes. The more I discovered my moment by moment need for Jesus, the more I could let go and know that even the ones who agitated my pioneer spirit also needed Jesus, just like me. The deep experience of liberation and freedom Jesus gave to me came when he etched in my mind that my struggles are not with flesh and blood. And guess what? Neither are yours. A truth that saves so much relational tension, wasted energy and unnecessary stress.

Deliverance from sin and death is not relegated to a formal pardon by an action or documented decree. Deliverance in Jesus is about connection to Jesus. Experiencing a conscious, tangible, radically dependent relationship with Jesus is the central message to this entire book. Please hear this loudly, clearly and in love.

Jesus wants you and me to remember – *"I am with you always, even to the end of the age."* Don't forget!

Reflection Questions

- In what ways does the Great Commission to make disciples challenge or overwhelm you? How does it excite you?
- As you reach out to love and serve others how do you experience the presence and power of Jesus?
- In what ways has your walk with Jesus been radical?
- How do you relate to Greg's reference to the lines from the Christian song *"Come Thou Fount?"*
- How do you recognize the presence of Jesus in your day-to-day walk? How do you respond?

Chapter 14 – Greg

What if Jesus Really Does Provide Us with His Rest?

Come to me, all you that are weary and are carrying heavy burdens, and I will give you rest. Take my yoke upon you, and learn from me; for I am gentle and humble in heart, and you will find rest for your souls.
Matthew 11:28-29 NRSVA

IN A RECENT CONVERSATION with one of our seasoned GCI Elders, Richard Andrews, the topic of rest in Christ became more real to me. Richard has been in the banking and finance world for all his working years. His present financial group recently branched off from one of the large national institutions, and Richard has been up to his eyeballs in regrouping, coordinating staff and simply getting re-established (all in the backdrop of coming out of COVID and the worst quarter in the Stock Market since 1970). Richard and I spent considerable time talking about the challenge through the chaos, even to the point of starting over with another job in another state. He categorized this time as a season of reflection and seeking the Lord's face. I joined him in this season to pray and seek wisdom from above.

Six weeks went by before Richard and I reconnected. I asked him what had changed? At work, nothing – it was still the same level of chaos and stress. But what had changed was Richard. He had an inexplicable newfound peace. A peace that had to originate in Jesus. He and I ventured back in time to the tumultuous boat ride of Jesus across the Sea of Galilee with the veteran fishermen.

On that day, when evening had come, he said to them, "Let us go across to the other side." And leaving the crowd behind, they took him with them in the boat, just as he was. Other boats were with him. A great gale arose, and the waves beat into the boat, so that the boat was already being swamped. But he was in the stern, asleep on the cushion; and they woke him up and said to him, "Teacher, do you not care that we are perishing?" He woke up and rebuked the wind, and said to the sea, "Peace! Be still!" Then the wind ceased, and there was a dead calm.

He said to them, "Why are you afraid? Have you still no faith?" And they were filled with great awe and said to one another, "Who then is this, that even the wind and the sea obey him?" (Mark 4:35-41 NRSVA)

There are several remarkable aspects about this story. First off, these fishermen had undoubtedly been in storms before. However, this particular storm unnerved them as they observed the boat filling with water and felt the effects of the strong winds. They thought this was the end of their natural lives.

Second point to consider is, where is Jesus? Jesus is curled up in the back of the boat sleeping like a baby. The disciples had to physically nudge him and awaken him. I envision him stretching and wiping the sleep out of his eyes then moving to the bow to assess the matter. Do you see him raising his arms to the sky and saying, "Peace, be still?" Then, the clouds dissipating, the winds calming and waves smoothing out. I imagine the disciples tightly huddled behind him and even clinging to his robe. The greater message of peace is not to the rain, wind and waves – it is to the troubled, fearful, lack of faith men who were his followers and friends.

I've heard it said that life is a series of events. There are times we are beginning the hopeful journey where all looks well and good, there are times when we are overtaken by a storm with the beating and battering, and there are times when we are coming out of the storm stronger for the journey. We are typically in one of these three stages and cyclically moving through each one as we begin the process over and over. The upside to the "peace of God that passes human understanding" is that it can live and thrive in all parts of the process. What?

Just like Richard was experiencing in the workplace, the storm continued for days and weeks and yet he was calmed, steadied and upheld by Jesus. He was experiencing the rest of Jesus even during toiling and bearing burdens (active and passive forms of oppression). These are weighty matters that literally feel like heavy weights upon your shoulders, and yet with the presence of Jesus and the peace he imparts, these yokes become light. And as Richard shared with me, because of resting in Jesus, he was able to serve and care for others around him.

This season of reflection for Richard and his wife Venida became a time of refocusing and empowerment. Instead of feeling the heaviness from the demands of the job, they became comforted and revived to the point of feeling charged up to look outside of themselves and to the needs of others. Seeing the workplace as a ministry field where the love and peace of Jesus can be shared is a wonderful flipping of the script.

Please understand that there are times when we need rest – cessation from activity and people. The Gospel accounts show times when Jesus got away from the crowds, and even from the disciples. I think one of his favorite spots of retreat was the home of the siblings – Martha, Mary and Lazarus. At this spot he could have the listening ear of Mary, and for sure Martha would bring some goodies from the kitchen (my personal commentary). You and I need to have spots where we can simply chill and not be pressured by life's unending demands. Having a hobby where you lose track of time is a great piece of advice for any person who carries the mantle of leadership.

The rest we are talking about in the context of this chapter is the calm confidence that Jesus provides by his presence in the believer. Once again, it is about letting go and letting God. He can carry weights that you and I can never budge, no matter how much we flex and strain. He graciously offers his rest and willingness to shoulder our burdens. May we graciously accept.

Concluding Thought

For many years I kept a print in my office of Jesus addressing the driving rain, the howling wind, and the white-capped waves. The print shows the remnants of the storm, but the dominance of the blue skies breaking in along with the light of the sun are testimony that the wind and the sea do obey this man called Jesus. If he can calm the wind and sea, surely, he can calm you and me.

I am proud to say that Michelle Fleming, GCI Communications and Media Director has this print hanging in her office. I pray that the calming presence of Jesus helps her cycle through the many stages of her journey.

Reflection Questions

- What causes you unrest? What are the heaviest burdens you carry?
- When is a time you have experienced the peace of God that surpasses human reasoning?
- As Richard and Venida were intentional in dedicating a season to seeking the Lord's guidance and will, in what ways are you intentional?

Chapter 15 – Mark

What if Jesus Really is the Head of the Church... and of Me?

Since we have now been justified by his blood, how much more shall we be saved from God's wrath through him! For if, while we were God's enemies, we were reconciled to him through the death of his Son, how much more, having been reconciled, shall we be saved through his life! Not only is this so, but we also boast in God through our Lord Jesus Christ, through whom we have now received reconciliation.
Romans 5:9-11 NIV

WHEN I TAKE TIME to really contemplate the hundreds, if not thousands of people who have come to me for help in either a pastoral or clinical way, the main issue seems to boil down to this – life for them is being experienced in a manner that is not "comfortable." Greg touches on this in Chapter 5.

So, what is uncomfortable? It can be anything from having unexpected expenses that challenge one's finances, to being violently abused (recently or historically), and finally taking the risk to understand how such an unspeakable, horrific experience has molded one into what they are today. There are many other ways that one can say life is not comfortable. For instance, one can say, "I didn't get my way," or "That hurt my feelings," or "That offended me," or "I feel out of control," or "They don't like me."

And then, there are the emotions one can experience making one feel their life is uncomfortable. Fear, anger, resentment, and disillusionment are just a few.

And finally, there are the "affects" (impacts of, or the way it made one change in behavior) of all of this. For example, one can become entitled and controlling, which can lead to one becoming demanding and narcissistic. Or one can become dependent on others to "fix" them. And one can simply be in denial of any problems whatsoever.

My point is this: if you are in pastoral ministry, and you sit down and talk with me about the complexities of human development, personality, IQ, EQ, defense mechanisms, personality disorders, mood disorders...the list goes on and on, you will become overwhelmed. So, what is all this comfortable and uncomfortable about...really?

You may be surprised to hear that scripture bluntly says it's just not as complicated as we make it out to be. Okay, it may not be that complicated, but I will tell you firsthand, it's impossible, until we learn to relate and trust in Jesus. And that, my friends, is why Greg and I have written this book. Jesus doesn't want us to get caught up in the complications; he wants us to get caught up in him. We can trust Jesus, who is the head of the church and of us, and this is Good News!

What Did Jesus REALLY Say

In Matthew 26, we read a verse in scripture that is usually overlooked. It's a statement that Jesus makes after Peter has cut the ear off a person who is working for the High Priest. We have all heard Jesus' response: "If you live by the sword you will die by the sword," and how his plan can't happen that way (through war and violence) or scripture will not be fulfilled. But the story doesn't end there. Not many preachers expound on the next couple verses, and in my opinion, they are profoundly important. They read as follows:

> *In that hour Jesus said to the crowd, "Am I leading a rebellion, that you have come out with swords and clubs to capture me? Every day I sat in the temple courts teaching, and you did not arrest me. But this has all taken place that the writings of the prophets might be fulfilled."* Then ALL THE DISCIPLES DESERTED HIM AND FLED *[Emphasis mine]. (Matthew 26:55-56 NIV)*

What just happened? Why did they ALL desert Jesus and run? At the risk of being redundant, I want to remind you of the two phrases I introduced you to at the beginning of this book. First, "You don't know, and you don't know that you don't know." And second, "Your response to a 'crisis' is more important than the 'crisis' itself." The disciples' responses to Jesus at this time are a classic example of these two phrases being experienced. And these two phrases are usually experienced, and "acted upon," when one's life is not comfortable, because what we expected is not going to happen...at all.

The disciples believed that Jesus was going to start a war that would overthrow the Romans and make Israel the kingdom it once was under David, Solomon, and the Maccabean Empire. But that is not what he came to do. He plainly asks, "Am I leading a rebellion...?" He is asking them, challenging them, to accept his plan. They needed to realize that his intentions had nothing to do with overthrowing human governments. He came to bring a new kingdom. His kingdom would make no sense to the human kingdoms of this earth, but it is a better kingdom. His kingdom is for all people – Jew and Gentile, male and female, slave and free. That means everyone.

"Doing" the Impossible

Earlier in the book of Matthew Jesus tells us a bit about this kingdom and how we are to look at all of humanity.

You have heard that it was said, "Love your neighbor and hate your enemy. But I tell you, love your enemies and pray for those who persecute you, that you may be children of your Father in heaven. He causes his sun to rise on the evil and the good, and sends rain on the righteous and the unrighteous. If you love those who love you, what reward will you get? Are not even the tax collectors doing that? And if you greet only your own people, what are you doing more than others? Do not even pagans do that? Be perfect, therefore, as your heavenly Father is perfect. (Matthew 5:43-58 NIV)

Remember, I said earlier, it's not that complicated. Even if it is impossible to do on our own. Fortunately, we don't have to.

Earlier in Matthew 5, we find the "Sermon on the Mount" where Jesus emphasizes that we are included no matter what we go through. If we are poor in spirit, we will inherit the kingdom. If we mourn, we will be comforted. If we are meek, we'll inherit the earth. If we hunger and thirst for righteousness, we will be filled. If we can then be merciful, we will be shown mercy. Pure in heart, we will see God. A peacemaker will be called a son of God. We are even told when we are persecuted for being righteous, ours is the kingdom of heaven. Jesus is telling us we live in that kingdom right now, but not fully.

If you recall the end of Chapter 8, Greg quoted Dr. Gary Deddo. If you go back and read that quote, you will see one very important concept. We only get a taste of the kingdom now. We will not experience its fullness until after we die. That is why the disciples ran away, abandoning Jesus and fleeing for their lives. They didn't know and didn't know they didn't know that Jesus was who he was, and since he was who he was, he could love the fallen world unconditionally. Jesus loved his enemies! Jesus loved their enemies.

Who are the enemies of Jesus? All of us were...is that sinking in...all of us. And what did he do for us despite us not even realizing we needed him to do it? He loved us; he loved our enemies; he died for all. Even while we were all sinners, even while we were his enemies, even though we didn't know we needed his love to actually fix the evil in the world, he loved us. This is where the disciples were. They responded as if they had an unsolvable crisis on their hands. Remember the second phrase: "Our response to a 'crisis' is more important than the 'crisis' itself."

You see, in my opinion, that is the "mystery" aspect of the gospel that Paul discusses. Why is this so important for us to consider?

Look at any situation that is considered a "crisis" in the human experience now – racism, sexism, social injustice, political corruption, war, famine, financial corruption, political differences, religious differences – the list goes on and on – and ask, how do we love those we believe are the cause of all these problems? Consider all the dynamics involved and ask how do we, as humans, learn to love those who are causing so many problems that hurt so many?

The Truth...

The truth is we really don't have it in us to love at that level, and Jesus understands that. So, here's my challenge to you. What if in the middle of all that we see as evil, someone is present, namely Jesus. He is the ultimate fixer. Notice I am not saying that Jesus agrees with all the evil and disruption we see, but he alone can fix it – in his time. He said the sun rises and sets on the evil and the good, and we are to love our enemies. So, here's a thought: What if that individual's evil ways will be their path to understand that they don't deserve to be loved, and despite their evil, they are. Wow! Can we start to trust that Jesus truly is in charge? Can we also see why Jesus' kingdom cannot be of this world?

Jesus' way often goes against all the "justice" of mankind. This tears at the hearts of those who experience so much pain and suffering – especially when it is at the hands of others. I believed my pain was so bad, I was entitled to make my own rules and live by them. I trusted myself more than I trusted Jesus – something I battle every day. The sad truth is, we love to compare our pain with others. We start wars when we think that another does not understand how much we deserve, and/or how much we have suffered. So, what are we to do with that?

The Answer...

Let's go back to those earlier passages in Matthew 5, the "Sermon on the Mount." Again, here we find the answer, and why Greg and I felt compelled to write this book. Read Matthew 5 again. Those who are "poor in spirit" and those who are "mourning" have hope. Remember, we wrote this book to help the leaders who are in churches today. We truly want to help you understand that when you are "poor in spirit" and "mourning" and, as I would put it, "feeling totally out of control," something miraculous is happening. You are living the Sermon on the Mount. This is what Jesus told his disciples they would experience; things aren't going to go your way, but that doesn't mean he isn't with you. He was also telling them what he would experience and cope with perfectly, so that the law would be kept perfectly and their sins – as well as all the sins of mankind – would be forgiven. How? By loving us and loving those that we feel should pay for the evil that has been done – especially for any evil that has been done to us personally. I truly believe that without God's help, a human simply cannot do this.

So, what if Jesus really is in charge of the church...and you. What if Jesus has a love so great that he is hoping and praying for the salvation of the ones that hurt us, abused us, and abandoned us. This is a love that is not found in our fallen state. And when we start considering that this may be at the heart of saving mankind, on one hand you will rejoice, but on the other you may begin to grieve. It will excite you and disillusion you. You will rejoice and you may get angry. You will experience joy and you may get depressed. You will be confused, and you'll start to consider how it may work.

But here's the best part. In the end, you will find resolution through it, and your heart mind and soul will be reconciled. With whom? May I suggest first with Father, Son, and Spirit, and then with your enemies. This is what I believe the Sermon on the Mount is all about. It reminds us we can truly trust that Jesus is who he says he is and that he is the head of the church and of you.

The disciples had the heart to eventually share this love with those that were their enemies, and they could not control whether their message was heard or not. The same is true for us. They participated with Jesus, while trusting him to do what he does best.

We do not need to fear the situations we find ourselves in, because he can be trusted to lead the church and lead us.

Yes, it can seem risky to trust Jesus, but when we do, we realize all our rules and defenses are no longer necessary. This that doesn't mean they will just instantly disappear; we grow in this trust.

We need Jesus because it is his grace that keeps us alive. In this way, he is even in charge of you and me. He is our hope – the only hope we have. And it is in his promise to "never leave nor forsake us" (despite our continued sins) that we keep pressing forward in this life of confusion and pain, and joy and happiness.

Paul gives us the greatest truth in Romans 8 and the main reason we can trust God to lead us and lead the church: His love never fails.

> *For I am convinced that neither death nor life, neither angels nor demons, neither the present nor the future, nor any powers, neither height nor depth, nor anything else in all creation, will be able to separate us from the love of God that is in Christ Jesus our Lord. (Romans 8:38-39 NIV)*

I believe Jesus can be fully trusted.
Need I say more?

Reflection Questions:

- What do you now know that you didn't know when starting this book?
- How are you better prepared to deal with the crisis in your life? In the lives of others?
- What are the good areas in your life where you are certain of God's goodness to you?
- What are the bad areas where Jesus showed up, or is showing up?

- Where are the messy areas where you are learning to trust him better?
- What would change if you truly trusted Jesus?

What if Jesus...

A Personal Postscript – Greg

Dear Leaders for the future of GCI,
There are certain foundational matters that have been raised across the pages of this book. As your current President and friend, I share these ideas with you not as a warning, but rather as some realities you will face many times over, and likely over again.

Authentic Christianity assures us Christ is present regardless of hardships and suffering.

There will be moments, even days and weeks when you ask the question, "Jesus where are you?" As the Psalmist of old stated, "I am worn out from my groaning. All night long I flood my bed with weeping and drench my couch with tears... How long O Lord?" (Psalm 6 paraphrased.) Just as Jacob wrestled through the night with Jesus, you too will have your struggles. You may walk with a limp for the remainder of your days, but if you are walking with the Lord, the limp will serve as a constant reminder of who he is.

Knowing Jesus through your shared sufferings is the depth of really coming to know Jesus. As you grow through the myriad of opportunities to experience the trials of human woes, you eventually change your questions to, "Jesus, what are you up to? What are you doing in this situation?" Undoubtedly it will be to fulfill something in you or me, or in the people around us. This is a new level in the relationship. Instead of feeling like a victim who is seeking deliverance, you are now more fully aware of Jesus being present in the circumstance and seeking to be in alignment with his good and perfect will.

Identity in Christ is non-negotiable. Any object, person, issue or even "noble cause" that comes in front of knowing Jesus is idolatry.

I especially draw attention to "noble causes" because they are a plenty. At the writing of this book the list includes racial, social, religious, political, gender, sexual, financial, environmental, and so on. Any of these have potential to be idolatrous if we are not careful.

The tricky part is how these areas are so real. They garner massive attention from the media and have incredible power to divide and affect us in personal ways. Even as a Christian believer, we can become so involved that the cause becomes our cause, and our identity gets swept up in the battle. If the cause becomes so central to who we are, and where we spend our time and energy, then being centered in Jesus is threatened. We simply cannot start with the cause and attempt to insert Jesus. We must always begin with Jesus and prayerfully and wisely join our hearts to what moves his heart.

Jesus consistently builds his church in all ages in all geopolitical settings. Those coming after us will have their generational issues to face. Remember - Christ is with you and in you.

All generations have their ways of thinking and being. The Boomers are concerned about what it true. The GenXers are concerned about what is authentic and real (kind of where I fall). Millennials are concerned about what is good. And then the GenZ are concerned about what is beautiful. Truth, authenticity, goodness and beauty are all important. Since we have the theme of asking "What if" questions – "What if Jesus brings all these virtues together in the life of his church?" And, "what if the church can live this out under the banner of Jesus?"

Society will continue to take you on a roller coaster ride with curveball issues that you don't see coming. It's okay. With Jesus in you, you can hit curveballs, sinkers, sliders, and even high fastballs.

Jesus will remain faithful to his headship of the church. How will the church be seen in the coming decades?

In chapter 13, I told you that the great challenge to the church of the 21st century is to overcome the negative stereotypes left by mine and Mark's generation. Sorry.

This turnaround can happen. It can only happen through Jesus as he transforms us into the inviting, alluring, positive and life-giving organism we are intended to be.

My dear proteges, the church must move beyond the inward Starbuck lounge, and social club mentality, and retake ownership of its mission to make genuine followers of Jesus. The church must foster such an environment that maturation in Christ is happening. So, your generation will need to have a sharper focus, and creative ideas for helping new believers develop a genuine, meaningful relationship with Jesus.

Take heart, Jesus is intimately and personally in the challenge with you and you with him. And it has been my experience to believe that you are created for great things in the Lord.

Support/Challenge Matrix

The philosophy of "High Support, High Challenge. Grace Always" has served us well. It was this teaching tool that attracted me to go on a deep dive with GiANT Worldwide™. The primary instruction I received was for GCI to somehow, by the power of the Holy Spirit, to intentionally move toward the quadrant of liberation. By his grace we have made significant progress.

My dear future leaders, you are custodians of the culture of GCI. You are caretakers and defenders of the culture, and even more importantly you need to be living examples and proponents of the team-based model of opportunity and empowerment that GCI has become.

What if Jesus...